Life Lessons from Stepping on a Toothpick

Short Term Loss...Long Term Gratitude

Kimberley Holly Curry

Susan

Source of Inspiration

Kimberley

Life Lessons from Stepping on a Toothpick

For more information visit: www.lifelessonsfrom.ca

Tellwell Talent
www.tellwell.ca

ISBN
978-1-77302-871-2 (Paperback)
978-1-77302-870-5 (eBook)

Table of Contents

Dedication

This book is dedicated to my son, Brandon Myles,
who has grown into a fine young man
worthy of emulation.

To my beloved friends and family who
helped me every step of the way.
Literally.

To my readers in helping make a dream come true.
Some of the proceeds from this book will be
used for my own philanthropy initiatives.
I've always wanted to help make the lives of
those less fortunate just a little bit easier.
In turn, I want them to pay it forward
and help others too.

And lastly, to my mischievous
and fun loving cat Jaguar.
Without you - there wouldn't be a story.
So purr on my friend...purr on.

Acknowledgements

It was through the help of many that got me through this personal tragedy. Without them I would not have fared as well as I did, nor found the inspiration to write about it.

Deep gratitude to all my friends and family who were truly part of this journey. Your comfort and encouragement helped me get through some very difficult days. Thank you momma bear and poppa bear for believing in my upcoming best seller status, because one day - it will be!

A special acknowledgement to my husband who really experienced this too. I did not suffer alone. Even when I wanted you to take a break, you never did, and were literally always by my side. I know you were just doing what you do, but it was rather extraordinary.

A special thanks to Katie and Trish who rearranged many things to help out around the home front. I recall with much gratitude all the ice packs, elevations, back rubs, bathroom help, meal making, hand holding, foot lifting, but mostly - those soft gentle smiles along the way.

And to my sister Ruth who shared medical expertise with me at a time when anxiety was high, hope was low, and surgery was imminent. Your calming and intelligent ways reassured me that it would all be okay somehow, someway. Thank you for the additional medical research and the collaboration with your colleagues in the lab too.

Special thanks to Frank and Bernice for always being right at the helm and ready to help in whatever way you could. Although that's your trademark, I experienced it first hand, and wouldn't have wanted to share my "Colloidal Silver" experience with anyone else.

All-embracing appreciation to all those who shared a handful of laughs when I was able to see the humour. For those who visited me at the hospital even when you were busy. For those who brought me meals, arranged the meals, lightened my load, adjusted my work schedule, took me to appointments, massaged my weary bones, helped me with dishes, help me to shower, helped me to shop, and even helped me to walk.

Praise and recognition to all the Doctors, Surgeons, Nurses, Homecare, and wonderful hospital staff, who although were doing "their jobs", did so with much kindness, compassion, and incredible cooperation.

Thanks to my friends Colleen and Jenny who read through the original first draft of the book, which was filled with a ton of superfluous thoughts, that at the time I thought was a good idea.
It was from you that I received my first literary compliments.

A shout out to all the book club reviews, opinion polls, and random solicitation. Your opinion and feedback mattered to me as a precursor to the big world of avid readers and insatiable critics out there.

And a warm and wonderful thank you to Carol who in the last home stretch was solicited for her opinion, not just for her wit and wisdom but for her magical ways of touching things as they turn to gold.

A concluding and very special
acknowledgement to Florence Christophers
for her editorial talent and expertise.
Your insight, passion, and inspiration were clearly
evident every step of the way.
To take such a draft manuscript and build
structural integrity into it the way that
you did, was sheer talent in action!
I am infinitely obliged to have borrowed your
gifted hands and warm heart
during this self-publishing journey.

Preface

There certainly is no shortage of advice out there on how we should appreciate each day and all the blessings in our inventory. The truth of the matter however, it seems to be more commonplace to take a lot for granted - including our health. We just get up and go every day and assume or expect that our body will carry us through to the next task at hand.

We assume that our heart will pump blood to all the right places, that our lungs will breathe in the necessary oxygen, and that our muscles will move us in whichever direction we choose to go. And for the most part, these very basic functions do happen according to the blueprint.

But what do we do and how do we react when all of a sudden we are faced with a limitation, a debilitation, a handicap, or the like? Are we easily defeated or graciously resilient? Do we immediately blame something or someone, or do we just observe and acknowledge? Do we lament too long or accept what is? Our own individual reactions are as unique as the situation itself.

There are so many variables in each circumstance, and of course, there is a time and place for everything. So my questioning is not to relegate the normal grieving process or adjusting to new circumstances, I am referring to long standing effects of events in our life. There are so many things that can go wrong, but there are so many things that can go right. Thankfully we have a lot of say in the outcome.

Closely behind the cliché that we should "be grateful for everything because tomorrow it could change" is the old adage that "it's not *what* happens to you, but how you *react* to what happens." Based on these two cornerstones of human resilience, I would like to share a brief story that validates these two statements and shows that they are time tested and true.

Until you are in those *exact* shoes - you may not *truly* know your ability to deal with specific events. You may not honestly know how *you* would bounce back from a particular adversity. When things are good in our life, we roll with it, and expect that every day thereafter will be the same. But things happen, accidents happen, big and small, things happen. I once read that adversity doesn't refine you, it exposes you. Seemed harsh at the time, but wise in hindsight. You really get to see your own true colours when the chips are down.

I endeavour to share my experience about how one small thing caused big inconveniences. How usually being "the person to help others", made it a challenge to be "the one who needed so much help." How choosing my response as I was convalescing at home, revealed areas of weakness that provided an opportunity for growth and development of my own individual personality.

Of course we want to believe that we have it all together and that our personality is very well developed for the most part. Perhaps we could assume this because we are at a certain age, are philanthropic, spiritually minded, have a certain career, or even a higher socioeconomic status. Perhaps we could think this because of whom our parents were, our associates are, or our list of impressive accomplishments. But the truth is, our personality can always improve. Research even states, that for the most part our IQ is fixed but our EQ is malleable. And that is good news on so many levels.

We can always tweak and adjust the nuances within ourselves to make us a better person, a better friend, a better colleague, a better family member and so forth.

Our genetic set point may be prescribed in our DNA, but the opportunity to improve ourselves is a ***recipe for potential!***

We can ask ourselves - who are we behind closed doors? Do we see a need for improvement or observe a trend needing some attention? Do we hear from others that we *should* change? Do we believe them? With the exception of perhaps pride, arrogance, or mental health issues, we should all want to obtain to such grace. To be the best person that we can be is such a noble and lofty goal that may very well take a lifetime of tenacity to achieve. But this endeavour of self-actualization may not come to fruition while basking in the "good times". A skilled sailor never learned from calm seas.

It is my sincere hope that you take away something from this story about how a simple thing like a toothpick became life changing. The lessons for me are still unfolding and I am still a work in progress.

If I wasn't saturated with imperfection and feeling the effects of everyday life in the 21st century, I might have already aspired to such introspection. But thankfully, there is still time and space to grow and learn…

"Lessons often come dressed up as detours and roadblocks"

Oprah Winfrey

Once upon a time on a beautiful summer Wednesday, I was working from my home office and had just completed a great conference call with Google. Yes, Google! To say the least, I was feeling pretty good about things. As I ended the call to one of the largest companies in the world, I smiled and thought of how our human resource services were perfect for their employees. As I contemplated next steps, I decided to freshen up my coffee and headed to the kitchen. After the Keurig did its thing, I added a few splashes of cream, and was ready to begin the proposal for them. Ahhhh, life was good!

As I journeyed back to my office down the carpeted hallway, I suddenly felt a sharp impact on the bottom of my right foot. Baffled by what it could be, I lifted my foot to get a good look.

To my great surprise, I just stepped on a toothpick! There it was, half in and half out. Seizing the moment, I attempted to remove it right then and right there. I placed my fingers firmly on the tip of the wooden splinter and gave it a firm pull. It resisted. I tried again. This time I was partially successful, but the toothpick broke off and the other half remained in my foot. Great! I figured I better sit down to try it again. I tippy toed back to my office where my beautiful fourteen year old niece was, to share in my surprise.

CHAPTER 1

A Thorn in My Flesh

After unsuccessfully attempting to remove the remainder of the toothpick, my niece offered to give it a try. Despite our best efforts and the use of every precision tool at our disposal, the remaining toothpick refused to budge. In fact, I think it was retreating further into my heel. It was then that I knew we would have to go to the nearest urgent care facility to get it out. Great! What an inconvenience! I was working, I was busy, and I had exciting plans on the horizon. There is never a good time for a bad accident.

As my niece and I packed up and headed for the clinic, I had one thought in my mind: "Okay, let's hurry up and get this done, so I can get back to work." Little did I know that what was about to transpire would lead me through a series of unexpected events.

In no time, my name was called and I was escorted into the room where minor surgeries, broken bones, and extractions were performed. It was clear that this room had the right tools to get the job done! I was relaxed and optimistic that I would be back home in no time, ready to resume my day's activities.

The first line of attack against the hidden toothpick – was a nurse who - before she even looked at my foot - forewarned me that foreign objects have a way of evading medical professionals. This however was quickly followed up with the reassurance that they would do the best they could. She got right to work. Roughly seven minutes later, she looked up with a defeated look on her face. "Hmmm..." she said, "I think I should call in the doctor on staff or refer you to a surgeon." I quickly replied "Oh, no, a surgeon won't be necessary. The doctor on staff is just fine. Let's just try this again with him."

After she left to go get him, I noticed that my optimistic mood shifted to a more cautionary mood and I found myself feeling the early tremor of concern. What if this doctor couldn't get it out? Would I really need to see a surgeon? Seemed ridiculous. Who has ever had to go to a surgeon to remove a toothpick? Would that *really* be necessary?

After a few minutes of anticipation, a middle aged male doctor strides in with a warm smile and beautiful accent. South African, I believe. I immediately felt relaxed and couldn't wait to share in his anticipated success. After a needle or two of local freezing, out came the high tech tools and away he went like a miner on a mission. After several attempts, he stopped. He had the same surprised look on his face. "The toothpick appears to have disappeared" he exclaimed!

Where could it have gone? Evidently it just decided - without any consultation - to recede further into my heel, hiding as it were from any offer of help. After a few more grunts and groans, he concluded that I definitely would have to see a surgeon. There was nothing more they could do. Sincere gratitude for their attempts preceded my referral to the surgeon the next day.

Fortunately for me, I was still accompanied by my niece who drove my car and kept me company. To show my appreciation, I offered to take her and my sister out for dinner that night. We chose a beautiful restaurant at a local golf course with a stunning view of the nearby Rocky Mountains. They were more picturesque than ever or perhaps I was just being more mindful. Our conversation turned to how bizarre this turn of events was and we unanimously concluded that it would soon be over. We surmised that more than likely what happened, was that our brand new baby kitten Jaguar found a toothpick and proceeded to play with it *in the hallway.* After her brief but fun interlude, she abandoned it and left it sticking upwards in the berber carpet before moving on to wreak havoc elsewhere. The fact that she left it at such an angle, at such a point in time, and on such a pathway, are all just ironies of circumstance. On second thought, perhaps it was the generic cat food that I had bought her the day before. One never *really* knows.

After an enjoyable dinner, I was eager to get home to tell my husband of my recent misadventure. His reaction was the best of all. His eyes widened, his mouth agape. "You what? Stepped on a toothpick? In the hallway? And half of it is still in your foot? "Yes" I said and quickly added, "*and* I have surgery tomorrow." We both shook our heads and laughed. What a crazy day.

CHAPTER 2

The 1st Surgery

The next morning, I checked my emails, took care of a few business matters, and then left for the hospital. I was eager to get going and get this situation resolved. Once in the surgery room, prepped and ready, I was informed yet again, that there was a possibility that they may not be able to extract the toothpick in the minor surgery clinic. They assured me that they would do everything possible for a successful outcome. This came as a complete surprise to me. Would I than be referred to major surgery? That couldn't be. My mind ruled that right out. I just focused on visions of an extracted toothpick and getting on my way. I adjusted my pastel green hospital gown and awaited the procedure with an attitude of fortitude.

The surgeon, along with his intern arrived and assessed the situation. Just as they were about to insert a long scary looking needle with freezing into my foot, I blurted out: "Could you please put that needle in *very* slowly? My foot is a little sore from yesterday with all that poking and prodding that happened at the urgent care clinic." He chuckled and said in a sarcastic tone, "Oh, so you would prefer a spa-like experience?" I smiled and said "Yes please!"

About ten minutes into the procedure, both the surgeon and the intern looked up and said at the exact same time "Wow!" Although they had the medical records from the previous clinic and were fully informed of what it was they were digging for, they were still surprised to find the other half of the imbedded toothpick! But they did and there it was!

The head surgeon looked at me incredulously and said; "How did you walk here?" "I didn't do it on my own", I replied. "I took full advantage of a hospital wheelchair and my tippy toe talent!"

The doctors proceeded to sew me up and wish me well. We were all in good moods. Things had gone well and I was now officially on the mend. I was ready to put this whole toothpick thing behind me.

Before I was sent home, I was given a prescription for antibiotics and for pain medication. "This is for pain control should you need help after the freezing wears off today," the doctor said. I thanked him and took the prescription. His final words to me were: "It should take approximately three to five months to completely heal." My brain went blank for a second from pure shock. Three to five months? Preposterous! How can a tiny thing like a toothpick cause such a long disruption? He must be building in a buffer, I thought, and began "fixin to leave" as the Southern folks say. I made sure to take a moment to thank him for his expertise and for successfully proving himself a match to the task.

After I was officially discharged, and with a few minutes to kill, I wandered about in the shopping district of the hospital. This was perhaps not the best thing to do when on drugs after surgery, I later came to realize. Nevertheless, after a few modest purchases of things I didn't even know I needed, I made my way to the front doors where my husband picked me up.

In that little period of time, the after effects of my surgery suddenly became painfully evident. In fact, as I was getting into the truck, it was as though the freezing medication in my foot shut off like a light switch. The last couple of days of 'digging' around seemed to hit me all at once. The sensation in my foot had crossed over from sharp pain (stepping on the toothpick), to mild discomfort, to tenderness, to outright torture! Incredible pain! I asked my husband if we could make a bee line for the pharmacy to fill my prescription. "Looks like I will be needing that sooner rather than later," I said. "Absolutely," he replied, and off we went.

The pharmacy we usually go to was close to our home and approximately forty five minutes from our present location. On this particular day, however, we were not likely to get there before sunset. We hit rush hour traffic, hit every red light, got stranded at a train crossing, and other such murphy laws that were in full effect! As our vehicle stopped and started and lurched, my pain intensified, getting darker and more sinister by the minute.

I tried to talk myself through it. I reminded myself that I had survived surgery before, not to mention labour! I focused on my breathing and coached myself saying that "It's not so bad. Just breathe. In and out. Let go of any resistance. In and out. You'll be at the pharmacy soon. It's all good," But this time was different - *really different!* These mental tactics were useless. This situation called for a pharmaceutical intervention, and fast!

Interestingly, and completely involuntarily, I began to cry. First, came the regular tears, then the big long alligator tears. Then some background music was added complete with sighing and moaning, which then escalated to begging to get somewhere, anywhere, quicker and faster. Please!

My poor husband was doing his best to comfort me with one hand and drive with the other through heavy southbound traffic, lights and train crossings. "We'll be there soon" he said with kindness. But for me, time became irrelevant. The word soon had no meaning to me. There was only the throbbing, wild, ice-pick like pain.

Our original plan was to pick up the pain medication at the pharmacy nearest our home, but we quickly devised a Plan B. We would stop at the brand new hospital on the outskirts before heading further south. It definitely seemed unusual to leave one hospital only to check into the very next one on the way home. I didn't care what they thought though, I couldn't drive one more minute. Not one!

CHAPTER 3

A Quick Pit Stop

After explaining my situation to the staff at Urgent Care, I was whisked away and given Morphine intravenously. I thought "Wow, these guys aren't kidding around!" Much to my surprise, the pain was only reduced by a modest increment. It went from 13/10 to a 7/10. Although that was better for sure, I thought that Morphine would take it *all* away. Any type of pain. Any day of the week. Anytime. I came to learn however that certain pain medication is better for some things but not for others. It depends on the injury, the dosage, the patient, and other such factors. It is not an exact science. One pill does *not* fit all. I wasn't much thrilled to learn either that the face and the feet are some of the most sensitive areas on the body. Great!

After an hour or so, I was ready to get going. The Morphine had finally managed to take the edge off my pain. I was able to regain my composure and put things back into perspective.

I thanked the staff for their support and thought of how hard the nurses and doctors work and how we have such an amazing medical system! Haven't we all had a moment when we were rescued from some calamity and were so grateful? Well, I can tell you, I sure was!

Interestingly (I learned from talking with the hospital staff there), that many people *don't* thank the doctors or nurses. In fact, more than a few complain. Sometimes about everything.

It got me thinking about how we can forget to thank each other. It's not just because we are preoccupied or in a hurry or in terrible pain, but rather because we don't take the time to notice the gift someone is giving us. The gift of their time, their kindness or their expertise. In the case of doctors or nurses, it may be their job to take care of us, but that is no reason to not properly thank them. To appreciate the gift that it is - they work to heal us.

CHAPTER 4

The Power of Gratitude

We have all heard about the power of gratitude and how it makes us happier, healthier, and more resilient. But at this juncture in my toothpick journey, it took hold in a new way. I knew it was polite to thank the medical support team and that is a great thing to do, but I also noticed how really *feeling* my thankfulness had the power to take me someplace deeper. Into the realm of gratitude…a state of consciousness, I have come to learn, has very potent powers. It has the power to crowd out our less desirable feelings such as fear, anger, worry and anxiety. It can come in and sweep clean our negative mental clutter.

I think I have pretty good manners and am good at saying thank you. But am I really good at *feeling* deep gratitude? Noticing the good in my life? In a *deep* way? I wanted to get better at this, which leads me to my first life lesson.

Life Lesson #1:

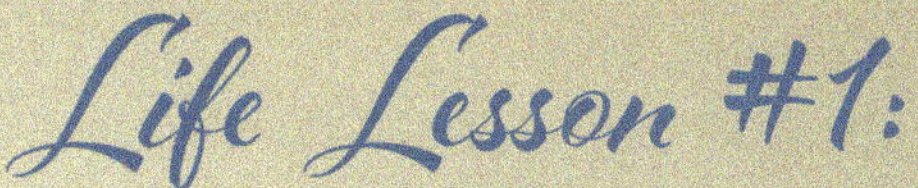

Really feeling gratitude and really expressing it to others, has the power to take us to a deeper level of being.

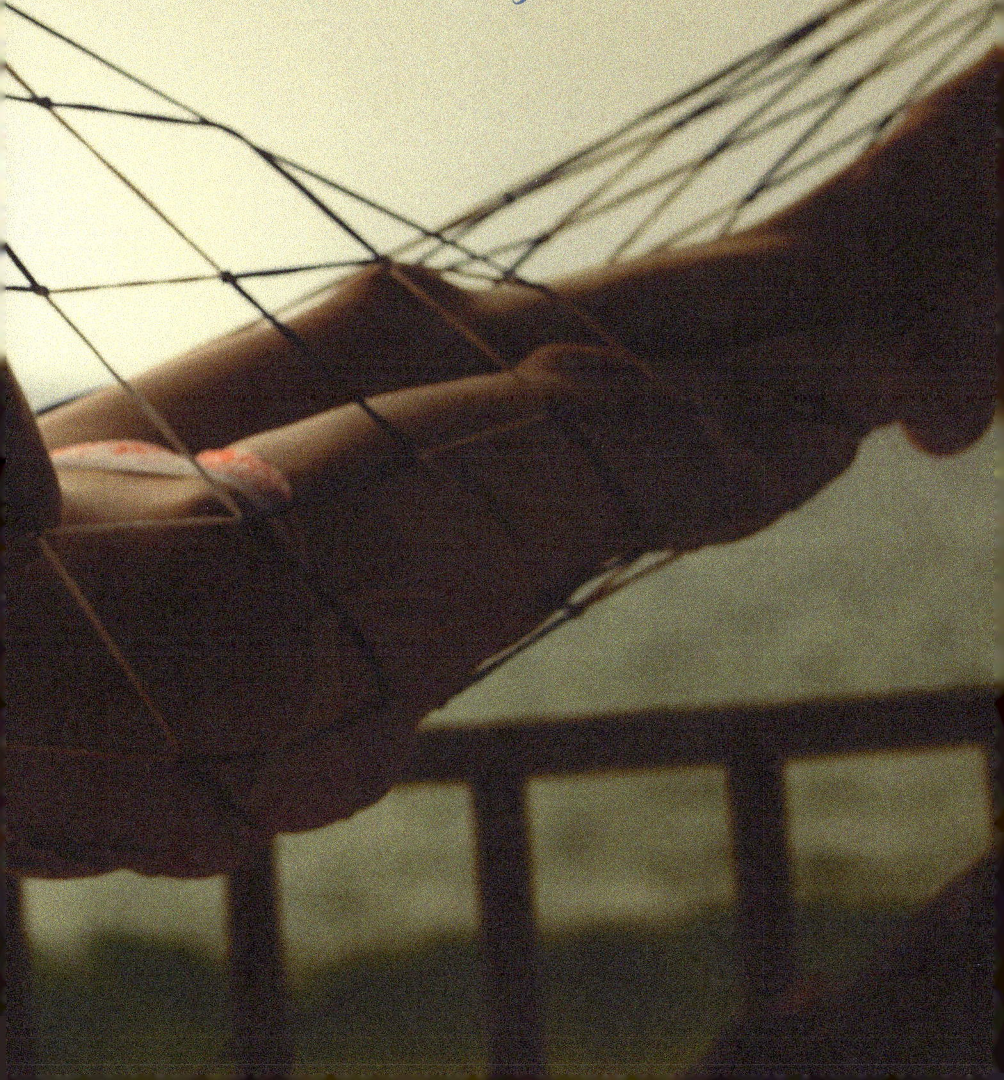

CHAPTER 5

Heading Home and On the Mend

Finally, we were back on the road and heading home. As we come around the corner to our house, we quickly realized that the eleven stairs outside and five stairs inside might present a challenge. Yikes! Happily, my husband (a great problem solver), drove right up the hill boldly mounting the steep grassy assent. He pulled on the handbrake and despite the steep incline, it held. That took care of the first eleven stairs.

The remaining five stairs were navigated together until at last - I was home! I immediately sat down in the lazy boy recliner and was greeted by our new furry feline. I let out a huge sigh of relief. "Thanks hun", I said to my husband, who was already heading back out the door to move the truck.

Later that night… as I was tucked into bed, I felt a warm rush of reassurance. Finally, it was over. The toothpick was out. I was now on the mend. I burrowed into the blankets and looked forward to things getting back to normal.

I woke up to a beautiful summer day. The birds were chirping, sun was shining, and the sky was crystal blue. I lingered in bed a bit to take it all in. I was feeling pretty good, all things considered. I happily anticipated getting caught up on a few things and resuming my work schedule right away.

Jaguar playing on the crutches - totally oblivious that she had anything to do with the "misplaced" toothpick

The first order of business, of course, was to master the art of mobility with my new crutches. This proved more challenging than I thought. I had memories of kids who broke their legs when I was in elementary school. They zipped around the halls and looked to be having so much fun. This was not my experience! It was a gong show. Hopping around the kitchen trying to make breakfast was almost disastrous. I thought cracking eggs with one hand was a feat. Alas, it became quickly apparent that I needed help and a lot of it! My sister and her daughter came to realize this too, so my niece volunteered to stay with me for a few days while I was getting the hang of things. How wonderful! This allowed me the opportunity to navigate around the house safely and to gradually implement a back to normal schedule. Working from home sure has its advantages in times like these.

As the days went by however, instead of feeling better, I was feeling worse. The pain in my foot was intensifying and I struggled to find comfort from ice packs, Percocet, antibiotics and elevation. I just kept thinking to myself "It has only been a few days since I arrived at home. This is just the healing process. Be patient." By day six, however, I was beside myself with unrelenting pain.

At this stage, I was *constantly* asking my husband and niece for a recycled ice pack from the freezer, and taking steady doses of pain killers. My sleep was interrupted by persistent pain. I also had occasional hot flashes, which I thought was perhaps just perimenopause.

Little did I know, I was having hot flashes because an infection was brewing – and a bad one at that! When that reality was confirmed, ironically I was relieved. At least

I wasn't in menopause - yet. The question then became, which of those two evils is worse?

Over the course of the next few days, the pain morphed into a constant all-consuming distraction. Rather than continuing to assume the best and think it was just the pain from healing, my husband and I decided to take a trip to urgent care to get it checked out. Am I ever glad we did!

CHAPTER 6

An Infection Brewing

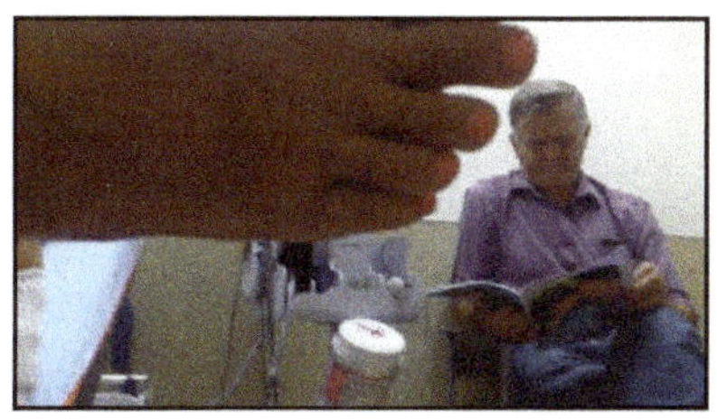

At one point, my foot was bigger than my husband - it's all perspective

After a short wait, a doctor examined my foot and ordered an ultrasound to see if there were any residual 'foreign objects' that would require re-opening the wound. The ultrasound didn't find any big foreign objects, so surgery was averted on that occasion. It did however confirm that there was an infection brewing. I remember a paramedic that was there who seemed frustrated by my requests for pain medication and said to me at one point "it's *just* a foot!" I didn't know if I was more surprised that he would actually say that, or if I believed he would feel the same if it was *his* foot. Nevertheless, I didn't dignify his comment with a response, but rather just hoped that he at least heard himself.

an IV pump was prescribed that I could operate from home. The pump gradually releases antibiotics just like the IV in the hospital would. What a brilliant invention that probably saves millions in the health care budget and prevents many overnight stays.

I returned the next morning to receive my home care training and brand new IV pump. Armed with my DIY pump and antibiotics, I headed home to fix this problem once and for all. And I mean once and for all!

See Image 1 in the Photo Gallery on page 156.

Seven days after the 1st Surgery- not looking too good

It felt good to be back at home. The plethora of errands, the days of unrelenting pain, the hassle of crutches, the chills and hot flashes were wiping me out. Upon arriving home, I finagled my way to my bedroom to lay down my weary head.

Unfortunately, a few minutes later I woke up. The pain had started up again. Sleep was out of the question. It was as though the pain itself was challenging my pain medication to a duel. "You're no match for me", it taunted. I was caught in the cross fire of this power struggle. I was baffled that the Morphine, Percocet, *and* IV antibiotics couldn't trump the power of the bacteria.

What else was there to do but start my cycle of ice-elevation-Percocet, ice-elevation-Percocet all over again? Unfortunately, I was quickly losing track of the amount of pain medication I was taking. I took it as "I" needed. Pretty simple. I knew that the maximum was twelve a day and didn't think that I was over the limit, but then again I wasn't really counting either. I was just trying to make it through to the next hour.

I was grateful that my husband and niece were there for me during this time and I thanked them for every bag of ice they brought in and for every pillow of elevation. I then apologized for every bag of ice they had to bring in and for every pillow that they had to plump up. At least my manners were intact, I think. Good to know one thing was intact, since everything else was falling apart, my normally high spirits included.

The next day my sister, who is a massage therapist, came over to give me a light massage and to see how we're all doing. This toothpick fiasco had become a family affair. I told her about the trip to the hospital the night before, my new IV pump and the pain medication that I was taking.

I told her that her loving daughter was bringing me ice packs at regular intervals and that she couldn't have her back.

She asked me how many pills I had taken since I got the prescription filled but I wasn't quite sure. She grabbed the bottle and started counting. After some quick math she proceeded to tell me that I had taken approximately 19 Percocet in about 26 hours. Ooops! We were all quite surprised. I wasn't just exhausted and in horrible pain, I was now in a very dangerous situation.

My sister left my bedroom to discuss things with my husband. Something wasn't sitting right with her. She had a foreboding feeling. Before long the two of them were calling the surgeon and updating him on my status. The doctor was flabbergasted that, first of all, I had taken so many Percocet and secondly that the hospital had sent me home the night before in that condition.

The doctor made a couple of quick calls and within minutes called back to say that I had an emergency surgery booked at 4:30 p.m. that day. My sister brought the phone to me and after the doctor expressed disapproval for the amount of pain medication I was taking, he proceeded to tell me that this was more serious than he thought and that I needed to go for another surgery right away. I tried to talk my way out of it. "Oh that's okay, I am just resting right now" I said,

"I have a new IV pump, new antibiotics, and it should all be good." He didn't have any part of it! He expressed grave concern over flesh eating disease and the possibility of losing my foot. "I assume you would not want to head in the direction of amputation, yes?" "Yes," I agreed and was appreciative for his plan of action, although stunned.

Surgery? *Another* surgery? This was getting downright ridiculous!

CHAPTER 7

The 2nd Surgery

I had a couple of hours before I needed to check into the hospital so I endeavoured to take a quick nap. But, just as my head hit the pillow, my mind flashed the words that the doctor just uttered "flesh eating disease." I had heard about it before and had a general idea of what it was but I made the mistake of grabbing my laptop and googling it. Don't ever do that! It was rather shocking and absolutely unbelievable what an infection can do. After scrolling down a few more pages of information, I called out to my husband that I was ready to go to the hospital anytime, even if it was bit early. All of a sudden I was eager to go to the hospital and end this nightmare once and for all. I needed the escalating horrors to be over with.

We packed up and prepared ourselves for surgery number two. I was comforted by my husband's ability to be very calm. It brought me peace. When I got to the hospital, I came to realize that getting an emergency surgery booked at 4:30 p.m. on a Friday night is quite significant and very much a privilege. I tried to adjust my attitude accordingly.

While the nurses were prepping me for surgery, my husband and I could hear the two surgeons talking in the background. One was the main surgeon, the other a student. They seemed relaxed and in good spirits. I felt tight and jangled. Time for me moved slowly. Seconds dragged on. I can still recall the contrast.

I was keen to get going, to get this over and done with. The room was cold and sterile and blindingly bright. I started to tremble a bit and breathe erratically. Fortunately, a lovely nurse with eyelashes like Snuffleupagus stepped in to comfort me. She brought me a warm blanket to help keep my anxiety in check.

At last the surgery got under way and I reached out to hold my husband's hand, (or should I say aggressively restrict the circulation to his fingers.) The doctors certainly didn't "break the ice". They got right down to business. They started by inserting long needles with local freezing into my badly swollen and infected foot. This procedure would hurt at the best of times, but sharp slivers of surgical steel were now piercing my raging, red and swollen tissue, and that was just over the top. One needle would have been bad enough, but there were many. The pain cannot be truly described.

I cried. I screamed. I gasped. I continued to squeeze my husband's hand until it turned a warm shade of blue. From then on, I was only allowed to squeeze one finger at a time, which he rotated on a regular basis. In the beginning he offered his whole hand, then just one finger, then alternating fingers. I was okay with that. It was the least I could do.

Like going to a dentist, I assumed the freezing procedure would be the worst part. It wasn't. It normally would have been the worst part but I *think* that the tissues were too swollen to absorb the full dose of the medication. I really don't understand why it didn't completely numb my foot, but more or less I felt the majority of the surgery. I felt the doctors poking, prodding, snipping and squeezing. I thought that was bad enough but what followed next was beyond disgusting. It was the release of the infection. My husband had the trauma of *seeing* it, whereas I just had the pleasure of *feeling* it.

To ensure that the entire infection was fully released, the doctors then applied strong pressure to various points on my foot. It was at that point that I became breathless.

I clearly remember gasping for air and crying to a deaf audience. They had to do this despite the fact that there was a desperate screaming woman lamenting beside them. The nurse kept saying "Look at me, focus on me" but it didn't help. I felt *so* alone despite having people all around me.

Within seconds of that last crescendo of pain, it was over. It was finally over. Twenty long minutes that seemed to stretch like the sand dunes of the Sahara. While the surgery was under way, the end was *never* in sight. The light was *never* at the end of the tunnel. My meta-mind had been hijacked. There was no me, no capacity to soothe myself, to think or imagine beyond this moment. It was trapped in eternity. This must be the moment when pain crosses over from something you can witness (I am in terrible pain) to something unbearable, to torture. When the rational mind is helpless against it, one is left with the pure experience of physical agony.

After I was cleaned, packed and stitched up, the surgeons approached the side of my gurney to say that it was a really good thing I came in today. They had just removed pockets of infection, and said that it was like "the size of two golf balls." They must be golfers I thought, and quickly converted it to a measurement I could relate to - about a half of a cup of infection - yikes!

See Image 2 in the Photo Gallery on page 156.

My foot didn't much like the 2nd surgery either

So that means that during the last week when I *assumed* that I was healing, the exact opposite was happening. Thank goodness that my sister and husband had the take charge instinct. This was very serious - I could have lost my whole foot! If the bacteria composition had of changed - I would have.

In my previous research flesh eating disease acts fast. It can ravage a body part and leave nothing but infection in its wake – all in a matter of hours.

According to the Centers for Disease Control and Prevention:

> "[A] serious bacterial infection that spreads rapidly and destroys the body's soft tissue. Commonly called a "flesh-eating infection" by the media, this rare disease can be caused by more than one type of bacteria. These include: A *Streptococcus, Klebsiella, Clostridium, E. coli, Staphylococcus aureus,* and *Aeromonas hydrophila,* among others."

Apparently you can have a *regular* infection and then for some reason the bacteria morphs into a deadly form and starts eating its own flesh. It happens fast. Even *E Coli* (which is relatively common) can undergo this transformation to flesh eating disease. Therefore, catching infections *before* they go mutant means time is of the essence. I was fortunate.

CHAPTER 8

My 1st Overnight Stay

Due to the severity of the infection, I was encouraged to spend a few days in the hospital while they monitored my foot. Before long, the concierge staff arrived, strapped me in and proceeded to wheel me to the ward where I would recuperate.

As I was are riding through the hospital on the stretcher, heading down long corridors, and in and out of elevators, that's the moment when I thought to myself: "Wow! This was *not* what I had planned for the weekend." Then again, I suppose there are not too many patients in the hospital that *plan* to be there unless it's a pre-arranged procedure. Hospitals for the most part are filled with good people experiencing bad things.

Another thought I had, which I hesitate to confess, was: "This is finally over. No more toothpick drama for me.

A few days in the hospital, a little R & R, and I will be up and at it in no time."

Little did I know.

When I arrived to my floor - to the unit - and to my room, I noticed that it was tucked in the back corner which was fine by me. I like corner offices, corner restaurant tables, corner anything. Everything is in front of you, it's like a bird's eye view. Not only did I get an ideal spot but my lovely neighbor was a beautiful elderly lady with a soft smile and shockingly frail figure. I said hello and introduced myself. Once settled in, I made a point of reassuring her that I would do my best to cope with the pain in the quietest way possible. She gently smiled as though this was perhaps the least of her worries. She had C.O.P.D. and was having troubles swallowing, breathing, and other things we take for granted.

So my husband and I settled down from all the activities, and we both were a little scared. He came over, sat on the edge of my bed and held my hand. We just looked at each other without saying anything. After a few minutes he ventured over to the nearby chair. We didn't have any words, we were speechless.

We *both* had been deeply affected by the last surgery. The screaming, the infection, the tremendous pain, and the horror of it all. It caught us off guard. It was hard to make sense of it all. We knew I had to have this surgery but we didn't expect "that". And we didn't expect that I would have to stay overnight either.

The experience of it stripped us of something I cannot explain. Maybe it was the stark reminder that life is full of surprises. You never know when some event can take you down. Perhaps these events help us savour the days when nothing bad happens. Maybe we will learn to be extra grateful for the uneventful days, finding basic goodness in them as they are.

After about an hour of resting lightly with my husband resting too, a feeling of calm finally came over me. I began to feel cautiously optimistic that this nightmare was now finally over. I mean seriously, what more could possibly go wrong? The toothpick was out. The infection gone. The foot saved. An amputation averted. All that remained was a speedy healing so that life could get back to normal. And that sounded good to me!

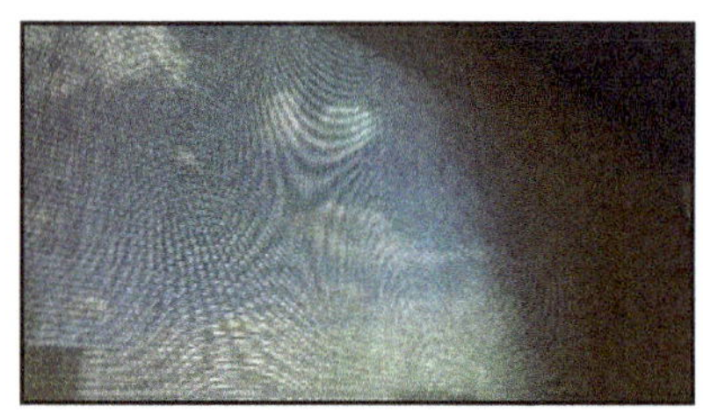

With the plethora of drugs you're taking-you start seeing things in the clouds that are probably not really there

As the freezing from the surgery wore off, I was medicated with Morphine and OxyContin. I have to tell you, this combination of medication worked wonders. It was much better than the last time when my husband and I were driving through rush hour traffic with *just a prescription* for pain medicine.

As visiting hours came to a close, my husband came over to tuck me in. "Good night hun. See you in the morning" he whispered. I watched him disappear past the pale pink curtain surrounding my bed and separating me from my roommate. As soon as he left, a sadness came over me. The reality of the day felt heavy but so were my eyelids. I fell asleep quite quickly and that was a good place to be.

I awoke to the familiar sounds of the hospital; the shift change at 7 a.m. with all the new staff and their new morning energy. The curtains were drawn, accompanied by a resounding "Good morning!" While you are still trying to decide if it *is* a good morning, you are thankful that the nurse says it is. No sooner do they take your vitals, than your breakfast arrives, followed by bathing care, and now you are all ready to go absolutely… nowhere. After all that incredible excitement to start the day, there wasn't much else to do but "take a siesta" as the Spanish say. Its sounds much better than – "take a nap".

No sooner had I nodded off, when I was aroused by the smell of fresh coffee. My husband was there with a smile on his face and a java in his hand. After chatting briefly, he left for work and I proceeded to go back to a state of semi-consciousness. Even though it was a narcotic induced state of meditation, it was peaceful there and I needed the quiet.

A couple of hours and a few *bizarre* dreams later, I was greeted by my sister and niece. What a pleasant surprise and their timing was perfect! No sooner had they arrived, when the last two surgeons came around the corner to check in on me. I was happy to see them and smiled and said hello. They smiled back but seemed distracted and somewhat apprehensive. This caused the three of us to remain silent. My sister and niece stepped discreetly off to the side while they unwrapped my foot to take a look. Their faces revealed nothing. Not only were they golfers, I concluded, but poker players too. Without further ado, they explained that a nurse would be right back to wrap it up and they would visit again tomorrow. I was grateful for their diligence.

The reason their timing was so good was that my foot was now exposed. No bandages to hide the toothpick crime scene. This left us with the burning question: Should we take a peek? My fourteen year old niece was the first to volunteer. I was amazed that she showed no trepidation. She proceeded to the end of the bed and bent down to take a good look. My sister and I eagerly awaited her reaction. After a few long seconds, she shot me a wide eyed look as if to say "Oh, you might not like this" and glanced over to her mother. My sister then headed down to the foot of the bed to check it out. She reacted immediately. She clasped her hand to her chest and said: "Well, they did say that there was a *hole* in your foot."

See Image 3 in the Photo Gallery on page 156.

Looking a little angry!

That got me curious! I took a deep breath, folded my leg over the other and stooped to see the sole of my foot. I was astonished! The hole was much bigger than I imagined both in circumference and depth!

It was a good reminder that infections are something to be afraid of. Not in a hypochondriac kind of way, but we need to be aware that if untreated, they can take away parts of our original anatomy in a matter of hours.

As I was carefully stretching my leg back to the foot of the bed, the words of my surgeon flashed to my mind. "Good news!" he exclaimed. "We cleaned up the infection. The bad news is - you now have a hole in your foot." I guess I didn't fully comprehend at the time that he *literally* meant a hole, a big hole in my foot!. It was the size of a Canadian dollar coin or loonie and about two inches deep at that particular time. I looked at my sister and niece and let out a long sigh. Will this injury ever cease to amaze me?

So this lovely practicum student comes in to follow up with me and proceeds to share that she had failed a couple of modules already and was pretty discouraged. So I reminded her of the three stages of learning; at first you are consciously incompetent, then you become consciously competent, and then you become unconsciously competent. You could tell that it resonated with her right away by the smile in her eyes. It was a good reminder that she is "just learning" right now, and these are all "just growing pains" so to speak.

Without any apprehension, she wheels over the trolley full of supplies ready to begin the task. I always wondered why they *pack* a wound and came to understand that if they didn't fill it with material, then the outside of the wound would close over and the inside might not heal properly. *Interesting*, I thought. Why wouldn't the body fill in the hole at the same time that it closes the wound? I guess healing takes its own time and the body is trying to protect you.

After I was cleaned up and my wound was packed and bandaged, my sister, niece and I enjoyed a nice lunch together and shared some good laughs. At one point in time, I laughed so hard I accidentally wet myself. This required that I be taken to the shower room to be hosed off in my wheelchair by my self-sacrificing sister. Quite frankly, we both had to laugh as it felt like a car wash. Nothing like the synergy of family to give you something to laugh about.

As I nestled into bed that night, I recalled a humorous expression that says "due to worsening economic conditions, the light at the end of the tunnel has been turned off." I quickly translated that to "due to worsening health conditions…" but glad that my light was now turned off because I needed a good night sleep!

CHAPTER 9

Settling In

Three nights had passed. It was now Monday morning and I knew I had to call my boss.

I wasn't quite sure what to say to him. The optimistic part of me wanted to say I was on the mend and that I will be back in the saddle any day. But with the way things had been going, that didn't seem quite right. Instead, I explained the recent emergency surgery, my current incapacitation in the hospital, and promised to touch base in a few days. He was so accommodating and genuinely took the time to ask how I was feeling. He also shared an interesting detail with me. He said that our minds will remember the accident of course, but never the *actual* level of pain that we experience. That might explain why some women have lots of kids - they have a short memory! It was timely and comforting to know that, especially after this last surgery! He was always sharing interesting tidbits of information like that. A truly wonderful person, that I was very fortunate to have as a boss.

A few hours later, my husband greeted me with a warm smile and fresh coffee. He wasn't looking too good though. He was feeling pretty distressed and clearly hadn't slept well. We just held each other, knowing that time would have to take care of this one for us. We have gone through some tough times before, so this too would pass.

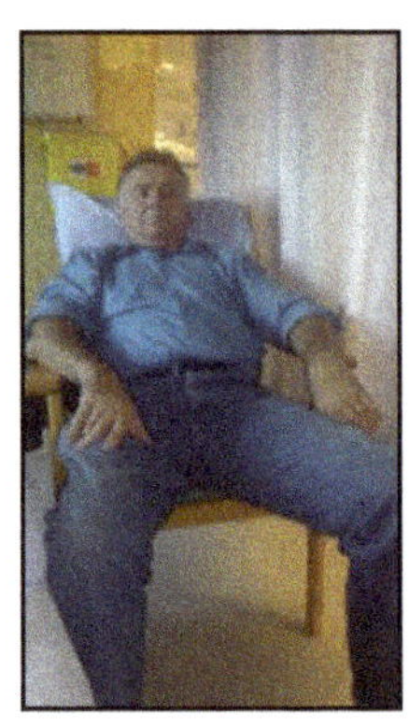

Tired-yes indeed! But there every single day

In fact this was not the most challenging thing we had gone through, but there was something unusual about how it was impacting us. I was well aware that some accidents are ten times worse than this one, or a hundred times worse, even a thousand. Considering that 1.3 million people die in car accidents alone *each year* and that 20 – 50 million become injured or disabled, clearly testifies to the enormity of tragedies out there. I know that each and every one of us experiences trials and tribulations. No one is immune. I think the thing that made this so extraordinary for us, was that it was such a *small* thing that happened, yet, the consequences were so *big*. It wasn't the magnitude but the irony that was incomprehensible.

As another two days in the hospital passed, I took the time to get to know my roommate better. She was well into her eighties and told me that because of her Chronic Obstructive Pulmonary Disease, her lungs were shutting down. She had trouble breathing and swallowing and it was dangerous for her to be home alone. She had been at the hospital for a few months already but said that she anticipated recovery every single day. How resilient and optimistic she was!

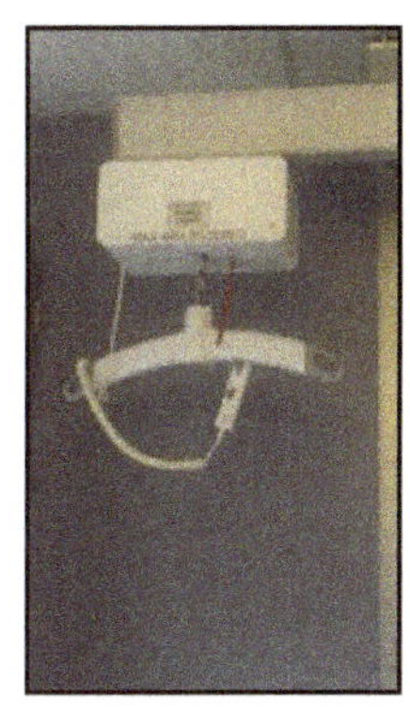

A quick look up to the hospital ceiling reminds you that things could always be worse!

On my fifth morning in the hospital, the doctors came around to check on me again. This time I did not greet them with a spontaneous smile. Not because I didn't want to, but because a sense of dread made my chest tighten. Just seeing them triggered the trauma of the past surgery where I felt so much of it. I was having a hard time getting a grip. Fear was flooding my body. Elevating my blood pressure. Making me feel hard of breath. In hindsight, I wondered if I was experiencing a post-traumatic stress reaction.

In recognition of this strong reaction *and* for some comic relief, I later joked about my condition which I named: PTTD (Post Traumatic *Toothpick* Disorder). Here is my definition: "A spontaneous fear of an unwelcomed presence of a toothpick in one's appendage and subsequent surgeries, infections, and hospitalizations."

This self-diagnosis reminded me of a time when I was a Realtor on an island off the BC coast, and would have open-houses on the weekends. It was often windy and sometimes rainy and putting out the signs and then tying balloons to them was a challenge. The balloons would tangle up and twist around and blow everywhere. If it was rainy *and* windy, then my hair would be drenched and my mascara would literally run down my face. Carrying umbrellas only complicated the process, as you could well imagine. One day I asked the team if they had any strategies to cope with this nuisance as I was clearly suffering from PTBD. Yes, you guessed it…"Post Traumatic *Balloon* Disorder." We had a few good laughs, brainstormed a few ideas, and came up with a workable solution.

Getting back to the surgeons who were busy examining my foot, they didn't look too happy. "Kim, I don't know how to break this to you," the head surgeon said. "But I am going to have to do another surgery. It's not looking good and the infection has spread and claimed more of your foot."

My body surged into overdrive. My fight or flight reaction hit the roof. I was freaking out. "The same surgery? The same procedure?" I stammered. The surgeon nodded. This is when I began to plead with them to do the surgery another way, with different pain medication or put me completely under. The last surgery was simply unbearable, I explained to him. I *cannot* go through that again.

The doctors understood my concerns but informed me in firm but kind words that there were no other options. This was minor surgery not a major operating room procedure. There wasn't much more they could do. They would be following proper protocol, which was the same protocol they followed before.

After they left the room, one of the nurses appeared from the background having heard our conversation. She proceeded to share her thoughts with me. She was a young petite brunette with sky blue eyes and a big bright smile. Generation Y is known for really speaking up for what they want and indeed she wasted no time in suggesting that we do exactly that.

"If you don't want to go through the same procedure as before, just speak up and make sure you are heard," she said like it was no big deal. "Let the doctors know what *you* want, and let them figure out a way to make that work." What I wanted was pain medication slightly less than the operating room with anesthetic, but more than the protocol for "minor" surgery. What I wanted was obviously something right between the two.

On their next visit, the following day, the doctors were surprised to see that I was *determined* to make my case. I did *not* want to repeat that same excruciating procedure, so if they could not give me adequate pain medication *before* the operation, then I would rather go home and take antibiotics for a year than have to go through 'that' again. I know that was unreasonable but that was how I felt at the time.

See Image 4 in the Photo Gallery on page 156.

Roses are red and feet are blue

As I advocated for myself, I recalled stories about amputations that were performed without any anaesthetic after the earthquake in Haiti. Not to mention the millions of men who suffered injuries and endured surgeries without any anesthetic during WWI and WWII. No wonder many came back with PTSD. But I quickly reminded myself that I am *not* on a battle field or in a third world country. I am in a state of the art hospital where we have medicine available, there is no political interference, no transportation challenges, and few budgetary issues. Surely we could find a way to get me through the next surgery without feeling traumatized. I made my case. They heard. They contemplated.

After they left, I proceeded to call my sister who is the Manager of Infectious Diseases for a Public Health Unit at a hospital in Ontario. I explained what had happened. I gave her the results of the bacteria report. They found; *Heavy Streptococcus Intermedius, Enterobacter Cloacae and Eikenella Corrodens.*

My sister made a few recommendations and suggested that I discuss them with the doctors which I did the next day. They said they would see what they could do. In the interim, panic set in. There was no guarantee. I was in limbo.

CHAPTER 10

Getting Creative

This situation inspired me to get creative or desperate (depends on how you look at it).

I started to research natural remedies to heal infections. I landed on a product called Colloidal Silver which is supposed to kill pathogenic bacteria. It was perfect! Just what I needed. I asked my husband to pick up a couple of gallons. He arrived with a few bottles instead. Shortly afterwards some good friends of ours came by to visit. We updated them on the details of our current predicament, then decided to go down a few floors to the visitors' lounge to discuss things further.

It was then that we cooked up a crazy plan of action. We would all pile into the public washroom and apply the natural remedy. We would work together to douse my foot with its magically suspended silver particles that had been shown to be bacteriostatic. I was not fully confident that it would be the miracle I was looking for, but I figured it couldn't hurt. These were desperate times calling for desperate measures! There is a time to be open minded and a time not to be open minded. This was a time to take action, and not be idle while the clock ticked toward another painful surgery.

Once the plan was made, things got even more entertaining. The four of us squeezed into a single visitors' washroom to get the job done. Once inside, I pulled out some random supplies that I had 'gathered' (okay, pilfered) to keep things sterile, and proceeded to unwrap my foot. It was tricky to do with four bodies in a small bathroom. Once I was in position, my foot exposed, my friend – who I affectionately called "Dr. Frank", with much patience and precision - proceeded to apply drop by drop the *exact* prescribed amount. No more and no less. This was in spite of my urgings to dump the whole bottle on it. The wound area seemed to absorb it but it did not miraculously close up. I guess some things take time.

Once my foot was re-wrapped, I stood upright, fixed my hair, and and rearranged my night gown. We stifled some laughs before the four of us casually walked out like nothing had happened. Like occupying the same single washroom was something we always did - together. No big deal. We had accomplished our "Colloidal Silver Mission" and were free now to venture on.

Later, we had to laugh. It was definitely a bright spot in our day. Harmless fun. While we were not likely to get the approval of the hospital staff for trying an over the counter natural remedy, we also knew that using it was benign at worse and miraculous at best. We were shooting for the latter. This, in and of itself, redirected my focus from dread to hope. For that I was grateful.

As our friends waved goodbye on the elevator, I realized how nice it was of them to come and visit. They took the time out of *their* busy schedules (and it was a busy time for them) just to say hello. They had to find the hospital, find the visitors' parking lot, find the ward I was on, and then find me. Note to self - whenever a friend or relative is in ill health, try to be more mindful of what they may need, whether it's a visit, a phone call, or even just a warm smile. It really makes a difference.

I have overlooked this act of kindness from time to time but came to realize that it makes you feel special when someone cares enough to put aside the inconvenience of it all, for the sake of spending time with you. It adds a little surprise to your day and shares in your circumstance. Definitely not something to underestimate. Herein lies my second life lesson…

Life Lesson #2:

Being more <u>mindful</u> and reaching out to those who are not well, is part of their medicine and part of their healing.

CHAPTER 11

The More - the Merrier

Soon after that adventurous visit, a couple more friends gifted me with their presence *and* presents. My one friend noticed my anxiety about the pending surgery and comforted me in her warm special way. Upon her departure, she left some bright cheerful flowers to remind me of her love. My other friend brought me a humorous card and some delectable chocolates. A winning combination!

When my son and his lovely girlfriend came for a visit, I was surprised to see him limping. Ironically, he was also nursing a foot injury, so we swapped sympathies. What are the chances? The only thing that was glaringly different about his injury was that his was due to a sporting accident. At least he was having fun. His story was exciting, where I *just* stepped on a toothpick. Surely I could come up with something more creative than that to tell everyone! Hmmmm.........

So one day, with some idle time, a friend and I brainstormed some *creative* versions of what happened. It was great fun. Here are a few of my favorites:

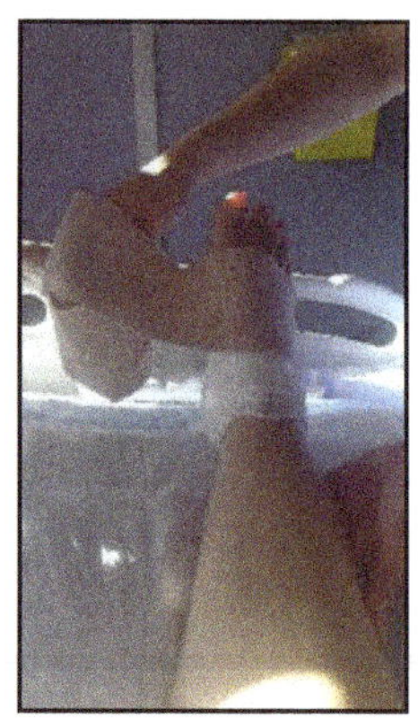

Round round we go

1. I was climbing a mountain to save some orphans. I fell off a cliff, landed in a tree and picked up a few slivers.

2. I was playing the "pick-up sticks" game with my grandson and forgot to put them away when we were done.

3. I was at a cocktail party with toothpicks and olives everywhere. I don't exactly remember what happened, but it was crazy!

A visitor reminded me to take time to "smell the roses"

As the week progressed, my nephew and brother in law came to visit. My nephew was all too eager to push the wheelchair and take me for a walk. "It's not as much fun as it looks" I assured him, but nevertheless, he grabbed the handles and off we went. He doesn't even realize how cool he is. And although my daughter in law had a jammed packed schedule, I was so happy that she brought our grandson by to visit along with a Starbucks Mocha-something for me to enjoy.

It was these special moments that helped to lighten my load and lift my spirits. They may seem to be small gestures, but in actuality they were quite big.

— CHAPTER 12 —

The 3rd Surgery!

Despite my best intentions to make my foot repel deadly bacteria by using Colloidal Silver, and to only think positive thoughts, another surgery was inevitable - whether I liked it or not.

The next day – surgery day - I found myself greeted bright and early by an entourage of surgeons and students on their morning rounds. They stated that they have come up with a solution and would be back to conduct surgery number *three!!!* I don't know if it was because I had just woken up, or the mention of surgery, or because there were five tall dark and handsome doctors at the foot of my bed (*before* I even had a chance to ruffle my feathers), but whatever it was - I was in a state of shock!

Left with jangled nerves, I remembered something I like to do in the morning. Just as I am waking up, I like to think of all the things I am grateful for. This seemed like as good a time as any to do that. It also fit in perfectly with my renewed interest in mastering the art of gratitude. I got right to work!

As I laid there pending *another* surgery, I began to count my blessings. This time my list was radically different. Now it consisted of things I normally take for granted such as my one functional foot, my tall stature, hot showers, clear mental faculties, the love and support of friends and family, having hope, and the game scrabble. Later as I listened to my roommate being guided through her swallowing exercises, I quickly added my ability to swallow to the list. I felt better already. I quickly concluded that "My cup was well filled!"

Ever since my friend introduced me to the concept of "Sacred Bookends", I try every morning and every night to do a little something for me. Sacred Bookends are different for everyone. Some people go out for an early morning walk. Some meditate at night to ground them. Some read the bible to get a spiritual perspective on things. Some put on a few of their favourite songs and dance like no one's watching. Some drink a litre of water and stretch. Some hit the gym. It doesn't matter. What does matter is that we start *and* end our day with some "private time" - gifting ourselves with some attention and self-care. The less time we have to do this, the more we actually need it.

Completing a morning routine is apparently the hallmark of highly successful and productive people. The book "What The Most Successful People Do Before Breakfast" details the research that validates this. I am not a morning person but I could see how this would create a feeling of control in your life, a stabilizing influence. It's a reminder to me that we have some control over what kind of day we are going to have. Starting off with positive thoughts and gratitude gives us a better chance of success, than if we just get up and go. It's the difference between being proactive and reactive. I need to work on that particular bookend a bit more.

As for the *end* of the day, that bookend is especially important and equally rich to the friend who taught me about the concept. She has an especially lovely routine as she heads to bed for the night. She lights bees wax candles (which smell divine), plays a sleep meditation CD, she states an affirmation, prays, and then does a little reading. Every night. Rare exceptions aside. It takes all of ten minutes for the routine, unless she has more time to indulge.

This leads to my next life lesson…

Life Lesson #3

Having "Sacred Bookends" in your life, <u>inspires</u> you to start the day and end the day in the best possible way.

So the reason I wanted to create 'Sacred Bookends' (though I would not have called it that - back then), was although I knew that appreciating the good things in life added a sparkle to the day, I didn't appreciate the importance of making it a *ritual* so to speak. I didn't know how helpful it would be to make it a regular part of my day, something that I could rely on no matter what was going on.

This whole toothpick dilemma was bringing to light my shortcomings about the way that I go about my day to day life. The way that "I roll". The way that I bounce back from adversity or challenges. It revealed the places where my ability to sustain suffering was underdeveloped. I was grateful for that revelation. I was growing because of this traumatic experience and there were life lessons to be learned here.

CHAPTER 13

The Show Must Go On

My surgery was set for later in the day. When my husband arrived, he rubbed my back with his "hard working carpenter hands", and although rough to the touch, it was somehow very comforting this time around. We braced ourselves for what was about to come. A third surgery.

It started with a flurry of activity. A ruckus outside my door. Then to my surprise, in walked two surgeons, a nurse, and various support staff. They got right to work. In no time at all, they completely transformed my half of the room into a minor surgery unit. They took the foot of the bed off, raised the bed to the highest level, brightened all of the lights, wrapped me well, and brought over the tools.

I was given something to relax as I was quite anxious. They proceeded to administer further medicine through the IV which helped with the freezing. I instinctively grasped for my husband's hand. Surgery number three was now underway.

I could not believe the difference with this surgery. I immediately noticed that although I could *see* the doctor digging inside my foot, I couldn't *feel* anything. Nothing actually. It was more than just a relief, it was incredible! I was undergoing another significant surgery without being in any pain. Now that was more like it!

In no time at all, it was done. Relieved and grateful, my husband and I sighed. "Phew it's finally over." We didn't mean the surgery but the whole fiasco. We suddenly burst out laughing! We had been saying *'it's finally over'* for days.

See Image 5 in the Photo Gallery on page 157.

Just one more surgery

I eventually came to understand that in minor surgery clinics, they do not have the manpower to administer pain medications like they do in an operating room. Their hands were tied during that second surgery. I was fortunate that the ward I was on supported this type of minor surgery along with extra support staff, so that they were able to give me better pain management before and after the surgical procedure.

After the surgery and before the nurses arrived to clean and wrap the wound, I took a good look at my foot. It was clean of infection and looked healthier, but the hole had become wider and deeper. They estimated the circumference to be about one and a quarter inches wide and approximately three to four inches deep. So it was like the size of a Canadian dollar loonie coin, and as deep as a roll of 25 of them. Shocking! Essentially, the infection was burrowing a hole right into my foot!. When the nurses returned, they cleaned, they wrapped, they left, and I slept.

CHAPTER 14

Finally On the Mend

In the days that followed that fantastically executed and painless surgery, I began to get stronger and more mobile. I learned how to master the wheelchair and my roommate learned how to swallow. I was both confident and relieved that the surgeries were behind me. I could now fully focus on healing and moving forward one step at a time. Literally.

Rolling into days eight and nine, I had to accept that the pain was constant. Although it was masked by the medication, it was still quite prevalent. I was getting tired, really tired. It takes a lot of energy to endure pain and I had been enduring for many days in a row now.

At one point, the wheel chair was taken away from me and replaced with a walker. Time for rehabilitation! It became my new found friend and foe at the same time. Not being able to put my foot flat on the ground meant that I had to hop. Believe it or not - that was exercise! My heart would beat so rapidly from just a single trip to the washroom. Hop, hop, hop, hop, this became my new gait. I was increasingly frustrated by how much work it was, to do even simple things like go to the washroom or take a shower.

At one point I became despondent, broke down and cried. My ability to walk freely had come down to using a walker and hopping everywhere. I admit - self-pity found a place within my soul. I began to loathe my situation and an ugly frustration consumed me. All my high fluting 'grateful' feelings were gone and I didn't even try to gather them back.

It was in these darker moments that I hid myself from the nursing staff, the hard working cafeteria workers, and even my roommate. I cried in secret and wrapped my face in the blankets, ashamed of my own self pity. I learned that you can cry quietly, but when you sniffle up your tears - that's not so quiet.

Although my handicap was temporary, it was still a handicap, and I was clearly feeling sorry for myself. I admitted that. I tried to think of others in worse situations who perhaps dealt with a permanent handicap. But minimizing my own suffering by focusing on others brought me little comfort. I actually felt worse. What I was feeling was a sense of loss. My *own* sense of loss with no comparison, no barometer, *just my very own loss.* It was real, it was raw, and it was all mine. I was trying to make room for it within myself, beside the pain, behind the drugs, and in between the sheer inconvenience of it all. But another part of me was resisting. It was slowly giving into the feeling that I was going down a dark valley. I wanted to take refuge in my usual life coping strategies such as praying, intellectualizing, eating, shopping, watching tv, or talking with my friends. Most of these strategies were now cut off and I was left to sit with myself – to sit with my pain. All this grief, sadness, frustration and powerlessness was consuming me! Not a good place to be.

Much as I resisted, I knew I had to make room for these big feelings, even if I had to move some things around inside of me. I knew I needed to do this in order to properly heal. These internal renovations *weren't* optional, as my usual 'coping' strategies were not working the same as they used to. I was forced to show up and be present with myself in ways I have rarely had to do. Which leads to my fourth life lesson…

Life Lesson #4

I've learned that its okay to sit with your feelings and to sit with your pain, as they are there for a reason. Just don't stay there too long.

CHAPTER 15

Getting My Perspective

As the days progressed, my healing finally turned a corner. There was no further talk of surgery.

Next up was physiotherapy. I had never been to a physio clinic before and it became quickly apparent that there were many worse injuries than mine. Although I knew this, I didn't expect to witness so much of it. I saw many patients without arms and legs and I watched them strengthening whatever was left, however best they could.

My Physiotherapist began assessing my limitations. She asked what happened and at first I got it mixed up and said that I stepped on a" Q-tip" ... Oh, I meant a toothpick! We

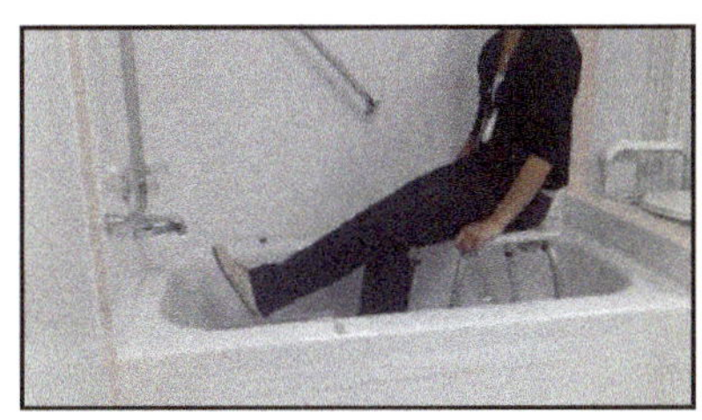

That was not the kind of bath I was envisioning!

enjoyed a little comic relief before she started teaching me how to use crutches properly. Who knew there is a right way, a wrong way, a risky way and a safe way to use them? Go figure. After these illuminating instructions and some physio exercises, I found myself blurting out "So when do you think I will be able to walk again?" It was such a strange moment. My question even took me by surprise. Reality hit me right then and there. First, I would need to learn how to walk without using my injured foot, then slowly over time with my injured foot, and then finally with a healed foot and then both. If I had any notion that recovery would come quickly, that was now shattered.

Approaching the end of my hospital stay, I was given a rare opportunity to meet up with other patients who shared their stories of loss and suffering. I was surprised by how many incidents of infection, struggles with healing, and random freak accidents that I heard about. A theme began to emerge, one that inspired me to write this book. All the pictures I had taken, observations I had made, and people I had

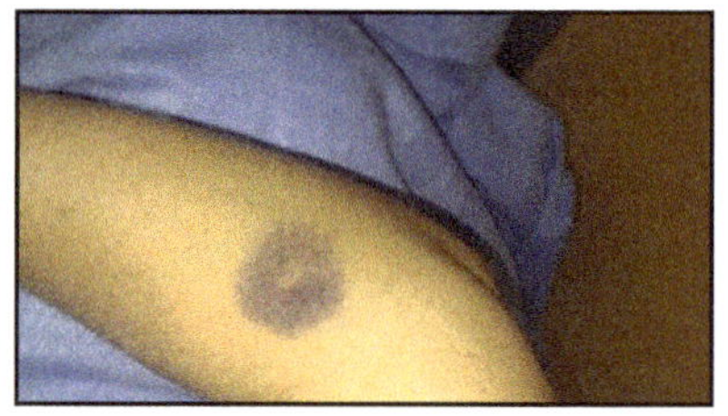

I clearly did NOT want any more needles

met, started to become a "collection" of data that would possibly culminate into a story one day.

There was one experience I heard that sat me straight up and straight out of my misery. It was as though I was shaken to the core and the scales of self-pity fell to the ground and were replaced by a renewed spirit of gratitude.

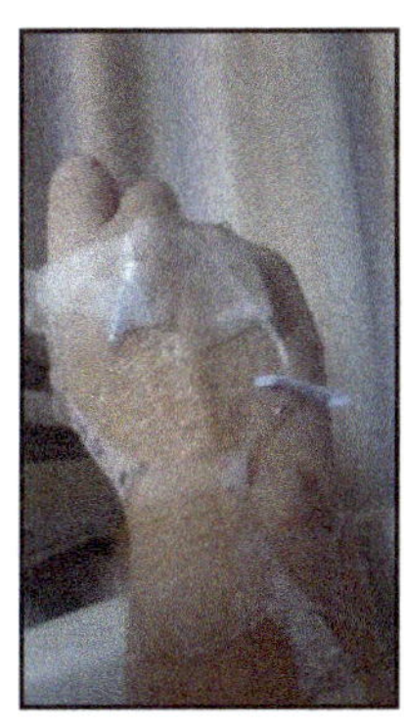
But I got them anyways!

It was a story about the southern Alberta floods that had taken place just weeks earlier. One day, while doing her rounds, a nurse happened to notice that I was in a bad place and started up a conversation, perhaps to help get my mind off my own troubles for a while. In the course of our conversation she told me the following incredible story.

One day she was helping relatives plan a beloved family member's funeral. This is normally a sad but relatively straightforward thing to do. However, just as all the arrangements had been made and everything was in place, a flash flood swept into the small town of High River, Alberta where their family lived. The waters rose so fast and high that the town was under so much water in the blink of an eye. It was like a tsunami had hit the shores of a prairie town out of nowhere. In actual fact it affected the entire system of watersheds in southern Alberta claiming lives and displacing approximately 100,000 people in the nearby regions.

According to Wikipedia in 2013:

> *"A total of 32 states of local emergency were declared and 28 emergency operations centres were activated. Some 2,200 Canadian Forces troops were deployed to help in flooded areas. Total damage estimates exceeded C$5 billion and in terms of insurable damages, is the costliest disaster in Canadian history at $1.7 billion."*

In High River, the flood spared few and traumatized many. It wiped out homes, family heirlooms, personal belongings, livelihoods, and a ton of local businesses. This nurse and her family were not spared. The funeral home they had booked was under water and severely damaged. Later they discovered, to their horror, that the graveyard where they had planned to have this family member buried had also been flooded. Having a burial beside other family plots was out of the question. Indefinitely.

It didn't take long to realize the scope of the challenges this family faced while trying to bury their family member. I cried a few tears of compassion for her. She said they were still researching other solutions but not without distress.

This conversation was sobering. I was reminded that suffering is universal and mine wasn't unique. In fact, who 'isn't' experiencing challenges right now? Almost every day? Parenting, aging, work, finances, health, relationships. We are all bombarded with challenges and some are quite significant like the Great Alberta Floods of 2013 that affected thousands of people. As I was emerging from my own crisis and merging with the world outside, I was surrounded by stories of loss. Mine, the least of them.

I recalled too when an elderly friend of mine shared that she had been married for over sixty years and everything she ever owned was claimed by the flood. Her home, every stitch of clothing, photos, everything. All of it gone! "I have nothing after 60 years…nothing" she lamented. I didn't know what to say but that I was *truly* sorry for all that she had lost and then gave her a big warm hug straight from the heart. Sometimes silence has more eloquence than speech.

During the flood, there was another family I knew that lost their business on the main floor, their residence above, and two vehicles - all within a few minutes of the flood hitting their town. They had built a thriving family business with their own bare hands and had worked very hard for everything they owned. Everything came tumbling down that day. It can take years to build something and sadly, just minutes to lose it all.

In addition to the stories of flood victims and patients while at the hospital, I also heard a few crazy stories while waiting in the waiting rooms. One such story was of a woman who put a boiled egg in the microwave to heat it up for lunch. Upon biting into it, the egg exploded in her mouth. The heated egg fragments burned the inside of her mouth which formed little blisters. These later became infected. Imagine that nightmare!

See Image 6 in the Photo Gallery on page 157.

She wasn't expecting that after cleaning!

Another story was of a most wonderful woman who was cleaning an older home after tenants had moved out. She felt a sharp piercing pain on her left hand but just kept working until the pain became intolerable. She went to the hospital where they hooked her up to an IV but upon returning home, she became unconscious. The next thing she knows she woke up from a coma on life support almost four days later! She said that her lungs had filled with water, there was some internal bleeding, her veins were infected, and they explained afterwards that due to the infection, she was very fortunate to have kept her arm. Years later, she is still unable to use that thumb. It was great to have kept that appendage, but she has absolutely no use of it at all. I reference her picture in the back "photo gallery" and really appreciate her sharing this very personal experience..

Then there was this lovely young lad who did the whole Australian travel thing, and while doing some construction work there, was bit by a spider. It became badly infected and burrowed a whole into his hand. He decided instead of having an ugly deep scar on the top of his hand, to put a tattoo of a spider over it! Now it becomes an artistic conversation piece. Brilliant!

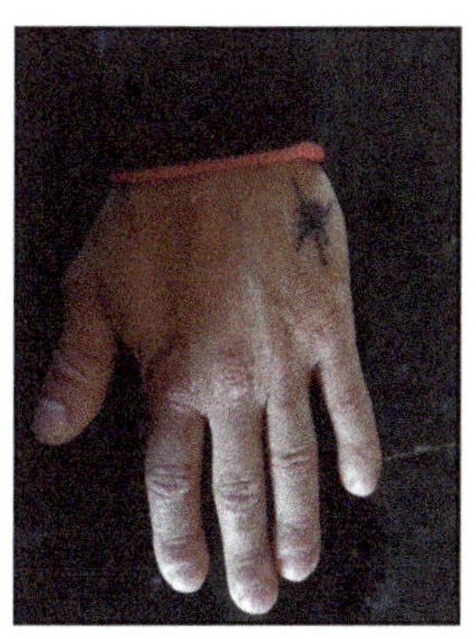

Creative way to hide the scar! See "Before" Image 7 in the Photo Gallery on Page 157

This traumatic story involved a man who had a stubborn and seemingly isolated infection in his big toe. Or so he thought. The doctors decided to surgically remove the toe but upon waking up post-surgery, he had no foot. The infection had spread and so they had to amputate his whole foot. Six months later they had to amputate below his knee and six months after that above his knee. Thereafter, they had to amputate the rest of the leg. And sadly he eventually had a heart attack. Unbelievable!

These various stories reminded me that when you get a cut or infection of any kind, to treat it right away. It is a portal into your body and if an infection spreads - watch out! Taking the time to put on Polysporin or some type of antiseptic spray and bandaging it up, is the least we can do to protect ourselves from the fury of infection. I came to learn that the formal chain of infection happens in just six easy steps; the infectious agent (pathogen), the reservoir host, the portal of exit, the route of transmission, the portal of entry, and finally the susceptible host (or the organism that accepts the pathogen). I don't recall *accepting* anything, but evidently we don't have a say.

On the lighter side of things, there was a friend of mine whose husband was helping around the house and ended up breaking two of his toes while vacuuming. A few weeks later he attempted to help out again and re-broke the same two toes! What are the odds? I assume that from then on, he only helped with the dishes.

What is one to make of all these random freak accidents?

Suffice it is to say, I have no answer. But I did find myself shifting my focus from being less concerned about how these accidents occurred and a little more interested in how people got through them. What inner strengths did they find? What new skills did they develop to see themselves through? What life lessons were *they* learning?

These stories and others that I heard along the way helped to put my own challenges into perspective. As I was preparing to leave the hospital, I was thinking to myself that it *really is* "mind over matter". It really is what we focus on that makes all the difference in the world.

Even if it sounds like a cliché - its good to look back at any of our challenging experiences and notice when the mind was in charge or when the matter was.

CHAPTER 16

Adios Amigos!

See Image 8 in the Photo Gallery on page 157.

Looking *almost* good to go

On the tenth day I woke up to a "get out of jail free card." I ate my breakfast, packed my bags, but skipped the coffee. I was excited to drop by Tim Hortons on my way home. I said goodbye to my fellow friends that I had met and to my favorite nurse Lynn. She was one of those nurses that, unbeknownst to her, spreads joy and radiates warmth by just being in her presence. She makes people feel hopeful, has an award winning smile, and a five star attitude. I was happy to have met her and the many other wonderful nurses who took such good care of me during my stay.

I also shared a few private words with my roommate, thanked her for her graciousness and wished her well in her ongoing recovery. Although our problems were at opposite ends of the body (her lungs and my foot) we endured the same type of frustrations. We were good together, and I was glad to have met her.

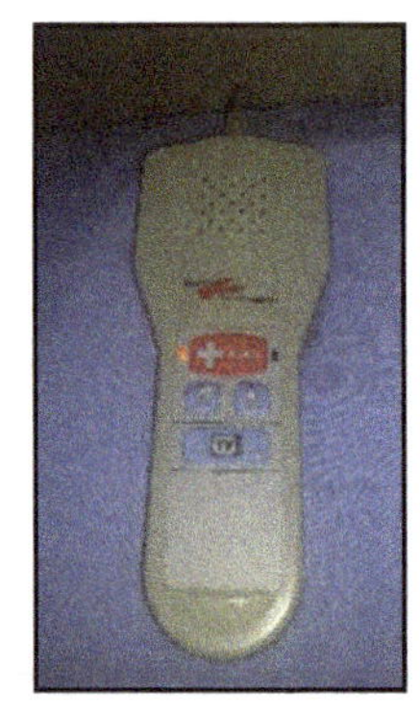

How privileged am I? If I need anything at all, I just push the red button

As we were getting ready to leave the hospital, I asked my husband if we could quickly stop at the flower shop before we go to get a little plant or some flowers for the nurse's station. He quickly agreed and off we went. The plethora of flowering options lead us to a unique cacti that was bright and hardy, just like the nurses. We returned shortly afterwards and brought it to their main desk. It was welcomed with much appreciation and delight and we thanked them for their great and wonderful care.

There was a doctor's tool kit in the hospital exhibit from the "good ole days"...not sure it was all good though

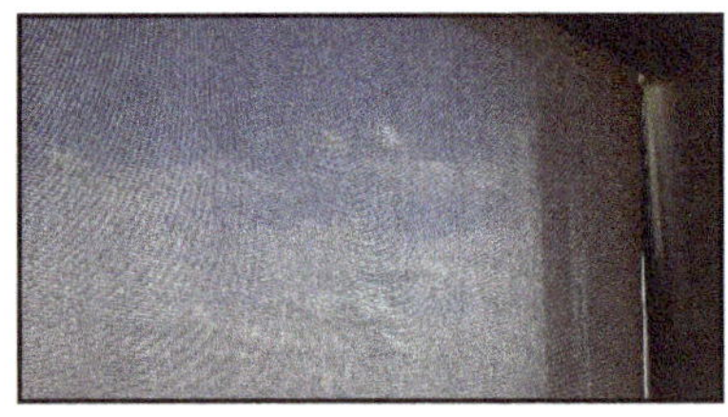

I swore there was something in those clouds!

CHAPTER 17

Help at the Homefront

The drive home gave me time to think about the months ahead. How was I going to build my life around this new convalescence? I was now mostly immobile. I would be inept in the kitchen, useless when it came to cleaning and grocery shopping, not to mention work. That was a lot to think about.

Low and behold, my deep thoughts were interrupted as my husband and I rounded the corner and our house came into sight. Those eleven steps were still there! Happily, just like before, my husband hit the gas and drove right up the hill to our front door. I was thrilled. One less obstacle between me and my 'home sweet home'.

I have always been independent, self-directed, energetic and generally highly productive, but now I needed a lot of help, and that would be a big adjustment. I am known by my closest friends and family to be a caring person by nature and like to help others, but now I needed help and a lot of it too. I no longer had the freedom to rely exclusively on myself or even to lend a helping hand. I now needed help every day, with almost everything. Even with things I didn't think of, like going to the washroom for crying out loud. It seemed like everything became a family affair!

My kitten is there to greet me with a backscratcher-complete forgiveness ensues

Upon arriving home, word got out to my family and friends that I needed help. My local congregation banded together and shared my burden. Many families offered to bring a meal to help lighten the load. How wonderful! Several meals over several weeks were brought to us which made things much easier at the home front. We really enjoyed the visits of those who brought the meals too and felt as though it was an individually wrapped gift. Under these circumstances were some hidden blessings. I got to know many of them better, more intimately, and that was *not* a blessing in disguise!

As for my work responsibilities, I was taken very good care of. Obviously I needed some time off and my boss generously covered my pay periods until the short term disability insurance kicked in. He made concessions and other allowances and proved to be an exceptional employer during tough times. He had a business to run and no doubt was inconvenienced by my absence, but you would never know it. He minimized the impact and was *truly* there for me in my time of need. I was so fortunate to have such a gracious and caring boss. It's no wonder that his life is so successful.

One day, weeks after arriving home, I received a call asking if I still needed help with the meals. I was feeling guilty for all the help I had already received but the honest answer was - yes. I still needed help. Even making toast and coffee in the morning and hopping back and forth from cupboard to fridge to counter to the table and back, all proved to be like an advanced Zumba class. It left me winded and wiped out. I was thankful however that my niece who was doing home schooling at the time, stayed with me whenever she could, helped however she could, and always did so pleasantly. She is the kindest young lady I know.

Eventually, we weaned ourselves from this loving kindness and the meals started coming every other day, then just a few days a week, and so forth. It reminded me of a bible principle that "we must carry our *own* load of responsibility". No matter what we are dealing with in life, it is wise not to expect anything from others, but appreciate everything! Of course this needs to be balanced as we sometimes genuinely need help, but the connotation remains; guard against our *expectations* of others.

As the meals tapered off, I finished up my thank you cards and called those who brought a meal or lent a hand. There were so many to thank. Many of them took time out of their very busy lives in my time of need. The generosities included cooking, bathing, dishes, shopping, errands, doctor's visits, and even a desperately needed pedicure! It reminded me of a book entitled "The Five Love Languages" by Gary Chapman. In his extensive research he identifies five different ways we all show love *and* receive love predominantly. I know for me, I have always shown my love to others through "gifts", and I receive love best by "words of affirmation". It is such an insightful read as it truly is the "*language of the heart*". Some might misinterpret your motives but only because they don't know your innate love language or your intrinsic

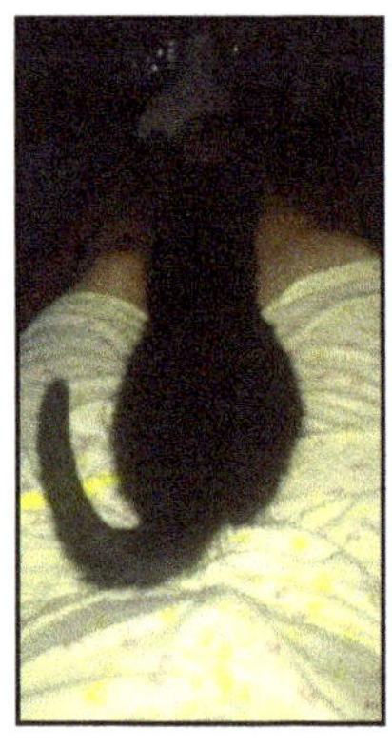

"Baby-jag" wasn't bothered by much of anything at all

motivation. Throughout this incredible journey, I got to see real love expressed through one or more of the five love languages; words of affirmation, gifts, quality time, physical touch, or acts of service. The variety of expressions truly *nourished* my soul.

With the passing of time, my foot was clearly getting better. As the pictures show at the back of the book, the miracle of healing was taking place before my very eyes. The body's ability to create new flesh and heal an open wound from the inside out, is truly a miracle. The body was continually laying down new tissue deep inside my foot; one layer at a time, one cell at a time, one day at a time. Sometimes when the pain was so intense, I would just visualize the actual process of healing that was going on inside my foot. Fascinating.

Popcorn is the cure for any human suffering, anytime-anywhere!

After about six weeks, I wanted to try and walk. Leaning into one crutch and releasing the other, I gingerly put my foot flat on the ground and tried to take a step. It was too soon. Just that one action pulled on the scar tissue which tore a little, bled a little, and hurt a lot! New skin grafting and repair would need to start all over again. During this time of healing, it was interesting to observe the passive judgements of some who would express disbelief that I wasn't walking yet. It was as though they knew something I didn't. It was at those moments that I realized the wisdom of not judging others because they had no idea about the specific complications involved in the healing process that was taking place in *my* foot. Furthermore, it was easy for them to say "just put your foot down and start walking" but in actuality it is counter intuitive to put your foot down, when there is an open bleeding wound. I knew what I was doing.

Eventually, I was able to resume a modified work schedule from my home office. And although I still had to contend with a plethora of drugs and their side effects, it felt good to be working again. I was grateful that during conference calls, I had a choice to just use the audio function, not the video. Heard and not seen - was good for me.

By the third month of being at home, mounting frustration was setting in. I knew I had to be patient and take baby steps on the path back to normal, but things were taking a lot longer than I expected. My patience was wearing thin.

CHAPTER 18

Getting Perspective (Again)

Despite many weeks of positive thinking, counting my blessings, receiving help, and resting well, I felt the emergence of frustration and impatience rising up in me. It would start as a slow simmer but then would bubble up to the surface. I was getting irritable and was *really* tired of this restriction. The healing was taking way too long. I-could-not-take-it-anymore!

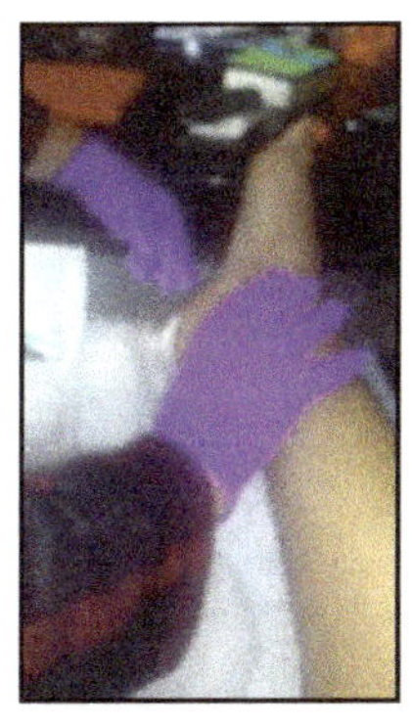

The Home Care Nurses were so kind, and patient. I looked forward to their smiles

I still needed help with so many things. I hadn't walked freely without crutches, walkers or wheelchairs in months. I recalled the movie "Planes, Trains, and Automobiles", and thought how mine was "Crutches, Walkers and Wheelchairs!" I hadn't driven for months, let alone go for a walk. I didn't have the freedom to just go for a coffee or even a movie with a friend without *a lot* of help. I was confined to my home and was becoming a shut-in.

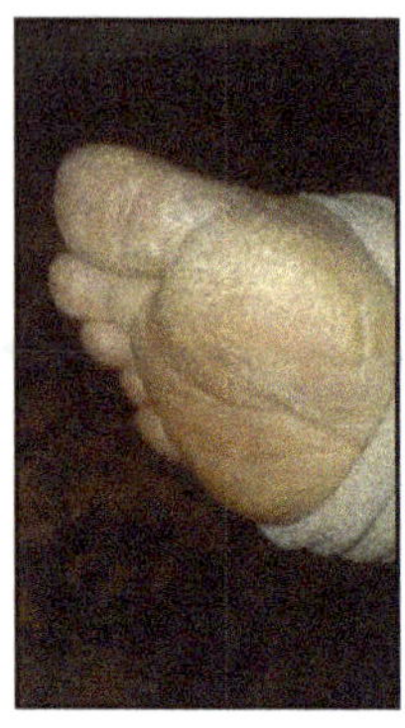
At one point a terrible drought set in

To make matters worse, the seasons were changing. It was now winter and getting very cold outside. The pain persisted and the meds were making me feel sick. Because of my cooking limitations, my husband and I tried to be content with eating anything fast or anything frozen. To add to the malaise and misery, the wonderful boss and company that I worked for had just lost a couple of big contracts and had to close down. So now I was also unemployed.

I was gaining weight from being inactive and was often feeling lethargic. All of this culminated in me feeling depressed and overwhelmed. Regretfully, the pity party was starting up again. This time though, I wanted to be ready for it - popcorn and all. This time, I was going to see it for what it really was: A life response that desperately needed upgrading!

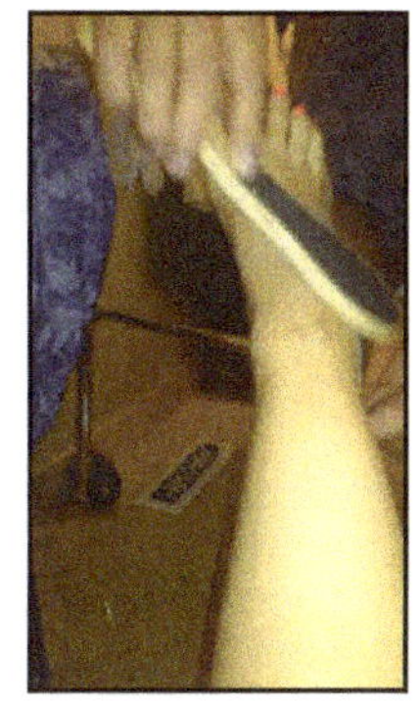

Out comes the aesthetician tools, although carpentry tools might have been quicker

See Image 9 in the Photo Gallery on page 158.

See Image 10 in the Photo Gallery on page 158.

Even my pedicure became a medical procedure!

CHAPTER 19

Breaking the Isolation

I decided to take an honest look at my life. At me. I set out to make a list of all the things I was unhappy about, all the things I resented or things I blamed for making me miserable. This was a powerful exercise. It became pretty clear and pretty quick that I saw myself as a victim. And equally unflattering, I was taking a passive role in my recovery!

Up until now, I had been *waiting* for time to do its magic. I was *waiting* for something to happen from outside of me. I was *waiting* until I felt better before stepping back into life. I had hit the pause button. I will be happy when… I will do this when… I will exercise again when… The answer was always, 'when my foot was better'. No kidding, I was beginning to resent how long it was taking my foot to heal. I had put my life completely on hold *waiting* for this one thing to happen.

The uncomfortable truth is, I didn't need to put everything on hold. Theoretically, I could have had fun with my crutches. Instead of feeling sorry for myself, I could have been hopping up and down the hallway with my crutches and getting into better shape than before my accident. But I didn't.

I could have exercised my arms or played my guitar more. I could have read more books and listened to more music. I could have meditated more. But I didn't. I was *waiting* for the miracle of healing to finish *before* I picked up and carried on, until picking up and carrying on felt easy and not so hard.

Why? Why did I let myself fall into such a slump? The unrelenting pain, being out of commission, the fact that I was now unemployed, still heavily medicated, tired, isolated, etc., didn't *fully* explain this reaction. It was something else. There was something more. Something I came to call my "Life Response Code". More on that later.

In an effort to tackle my mental list of resentments, I set out to take a more active role in making my life right. To stop making excuses for feeling terrible. To brainstorm solutions *and implement them.*

One place I started was breaking my isolation. I made some calls and set up some lunch and dinner dates. I cherished those visits even more than normal. It made a huge difference to get outside, to be around people, to feel the fresh air on my face, and to listen to the lives, interests, and stories of others. This one lovely friend shared stories of her two previous husbands and all their wonderful world travels. She has outlived them both sadly, but has done so very graciously. She is now left with just memories, but very wonderful ones that will last her beautiful lifetime!

One night my sister came over after a long hard week as a Massage Therapist. She took one look at me and said "You look like crap! Get up and get dressed. We are going out for dinner!" Admittedly, it was a hassle to get up, get dressed, get in and out of cars, and hobble around in the snow. But if I was serious about breaking out of my funk, I needed to extend the effort. We went to a beautiful authentic East Indian restaurant which is my favorite cuisine. The only rule was, that we couldn't order anything that we had tasted before. That was great! We tried many new dishes and mixed them all up. I have yet to try an East Indian dish that I don't like. So between the aroma of the spices, the delicious red wine, and the easy company of my sister, it made for a memorable evening.

This whole experience reminded me of the saying "people change either through inspiration or desperation." I was waiting for inspiration but in truth, it wasn't until desperation kicked in that I made some changes. Going forward, I wanted to do better. This was not the first, and would not be the last crisis I encounter. Falling into 'victim consciousness' after difficult times is not a pattern I wanted to perpetuate.

See Image 11 in the Photo Gallery on page 158.

Evidently keeping the wound dry is paramount to healing

There was a paradigm shift happening which was rousing on so many levels.

— CHAPTER 20 —

Life Response Code

Surprisingly, out of my suffering, festering frustration, and simmering feelings of self pity came a huge shift in attitude. I knew I wanted to respond *better* to challenges and to turn things around faster than I was doing with this experience. In the midst of all this misery, I started thinking about the QR Code that we see on a lot of products now. It stands for Quick Response Code and was originally designed for the automotive industry in Japan. This code uses four standardized encoding modes (numeric, alphanumeric, byte/binary, and kanji) to efficiently store data and allows you to scan the code and get a synopsis on the product or service, or it may even take you directly to their website. That one code contains the majority of information you need.

I thought about how I could apply that concept of "stored information" to life in the way of a LR Code, a "**Life Response Code**". After having gone through a significant challenge myself, I wondered how *others* would have responded. How are they wired? What do their encoding modes consist of? How have they learned to cope? How do their thoughts help or hinder them? Is it easier for them to remember the "bigger picture" when they suffer smaller things?

This concept of an LR Code was insightful to me. It was life changing! If I was 'scanned' so to speak, what would I see? What would others see? It motivated me to consider not just my circumstances, but rather my ***response*** to those circumstances. It inspired me to stand in the gap between the event *and* my reaction. It made me really look at my own private thoughts, my own internal dialogue, the assumptions I was making, and my beliefs about the situation.

Some of the things that came across my mind was; This is never going to end, I am so tired of this, This is so frustrating, Other people…, I am…, Why me, why then, why now?

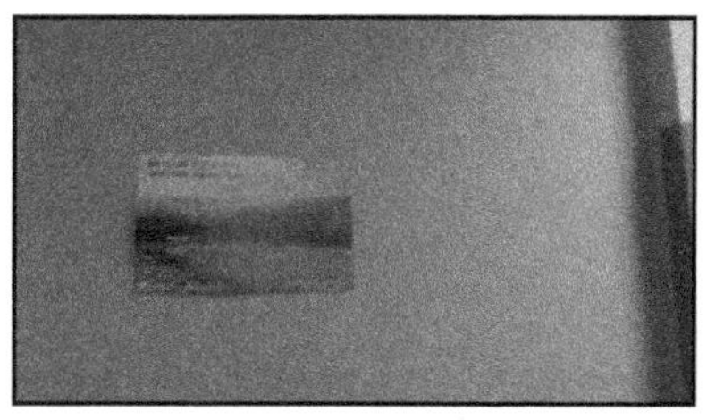

A hospital poster read "be mindful of drama and over significance" What a good reminder

Instead of dwelling on those thoughts, I was better off asking myself this ***one*** question:

"I wonder what good will come of this?"

When you ask a question your brain gets to work right away, trying to find an answer. This question in particular, directs our brain's energy towards the positive, the hidden gift, the "better than before" future that lies just ahead.

There is a saying: "What we think about, comes about." Up to this point, too much of my focus was on what *wasn't* working, what I *didn't* have, and what I *didn't* want. No surprise that instead of feeling better as the months lingered on, I felt worse.

At this juncture, though, the downward spiral started to change. I began to redirect my focus from what I had lost to what I could do. It was empowering. It neutralised my feelings of powerlessness, and provided me with a totally different trajectory.

During less favourable circumstances, I will try to remember to ask the question "I wonder what good will come of this?" It is so simple, yet so profound in terms of how it can shift your mindset. I noticed distinctly a paradigm shift in my way of thinking.

We have all heard of people coming out of the same terrible experience, but one goes on to do great things; starts foundations, helps others, lives a rewarding life, but another goes on to a life of addictions, self-abuse, apathy, and possibly even suicide.

What's the difference? How can there be two completely different outcomes from the exact same experience?

It might possibly come down to their individual LR Code and how they are wired. True, some wiring is inherent to the individual but some wiring can also be upgraded. Neuroplasticity has more than proven that. How we respond is far more under the purview of free will than genetic hardwiring. And that is good news!

This revelation was so inspiring that I wanted to design my own "LR Code" and trademark it, but then seen this clip art depicting the exact same image I envisioned. So what was my LR Code *before* this experience? What was it *afterwards*? It was not the same. I had undergone a transformation. The best way I know to describe it is to use the analogy of a 'vicious cycle' versus a 'virtuous cycle'.

CHAPTER 21

The Vicious & Virtuous Cycle

What is a vicious cycle, just exactly? Here is the official definition from the Urban Dictionary:

> A sequence of reciprocal cause and effect in which two or more elements intensify and aggravate each other, leading inexorably to a worsening of the situation.

Or

> A bad situation or behavior that is the cause of another situation (or causal chain) which in turn causes the first, bad situation again.

It is, in short, a feedback loop that keeps going around, making the problem worse. The only thing that stops this cycle is an intervention - something powerful enough to stop the spinning or change its polarity, making it spin in the opposite direction.

When I looked at my life while convalescing at home, it was clear to me that that's what I was in. A vicious cycle. I needed an intervention!

The intervention that I was hoping for however, was a speedy recovery (time would heal all wounds, make everything better). But the intervention that I really needed, was *not outside* of me, it was an *inside* job.

It was up to me to stop adding to the problem by neglecting myself, by being passive, by feeling sorry for myself. I needed to find a way to turn this negative event into something positive; to change its polarity. To have it spin in an upwards direction - into a Virtuous Cycle, where one good action leads to another, which leads to favourable outcomes, which leads to more favourable outcomes.

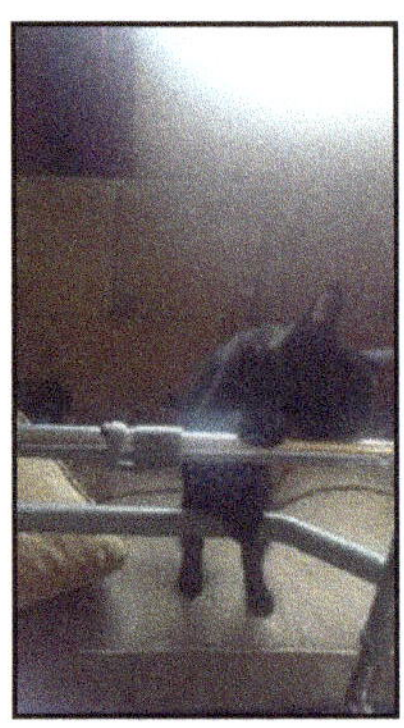

Even my cat was doing virtuous things by helping me with the walker

Here is the definition of a virtuous cycle from the Business Dictionary:

> A self-propagating advantageous situation in which a successful action leads to more of a desired result or another success which generates still more

desired results or successes in a chain. For example, compound interest earned on a deposit keeps on generating ever greater amounts of interest.

Another example is; if you eat better, you have more energy, you exercise more, you feel better, you work better, and you perform at a higher level. This leads to an increase in confidence, which leads to optimum performance… and on and on. Case in point.

How good our lives can get is unlimited. Just how bad it can get is also unlimited.

But for the most part-
she was pretty busy

I needed to make sure that the action I was taking, was taking me in the direction of the results I wanted. The book "Motivation Manifesto" captures the essence of motivation as a separate entity and in fact - it is. This leads me to my final and most significant life lesson…

Life Lesson #5

We need to take the action in order to get
the results we want, whether we feel like it or not.
Motivation comes after taking action,
rarely does it come before!

Here is an example of a vicious cycle and a virtuous cycle:

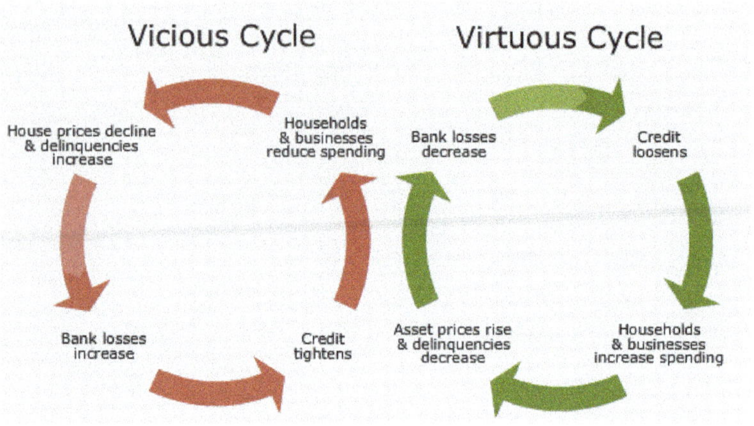

It was becoming quite clear. I needed to upgrade my Life Response Code from a vicious cycle point of view, to a virtuous one. Although I usually have a positive disposition, I needed to be *more mindful* and *practice* virtuous thoughts more consistently. I needed to flip the switch and get things spinning in an upward direction so the elements of my life would get better.

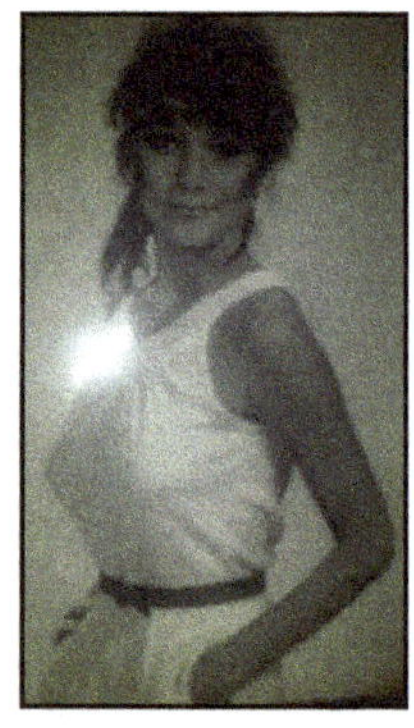

Looking back at pictures of when you were young, remind you that aging is mandatory, but growing old is optional

So learning to embrace the good thoughts more quickly, compounding them with other good thoughts and deeds, and getting intervention if you detect any faulty wiring early on in a trial, will contribute to healthier resilience, renewed energy, and a focus on virtuous things that can only get better with time.

Ironically, the Chinese have long known this. Have you ever seen their symbol for crisis? Interestingly, it is the exact same symbol as the one used for opportunity. It would be strange if you were reading a book and seen the symbol, but not knowing whether the author meant crisis *or* opportunity. Then in the course of trying to figure it out, you suddenly realize that they mean the exact same thing! Crisis *and* opportunity can be one and the same. Profound! What I needed to do was to find the opportunities inherent in my own crisis. To look at it less like a wall and more like a doorway.

In Chinese,
this symbol means
crisis **and** opportunity!

CHAPTER 22

Internal Renovations

It wasn't long after the LRC concept came to me that I began to turn things around. I was no longer the passive victim of a freak accident and a long recovery. I was slowly becoming a person in the process of intense personal growth, although I did have to pace myself.

My biggest "pacing" lesson came one day when I just *wanted* to go grocery shopping like everyone else does! So I meandered my way to the grocery store and was determined to go and get a handful of things *without* the use of a motorized wheelchair. Well, the first ten minutes was pretty good, but then I found myself in the middle of the grocery store with a full hand held basket and a throbbing foot. I recall looking down a long 950 foot aisle wondering, how will I ever make it back there. It was then that I learned the value of baby steps. Start small.

In the early months of the new year, I could see solid signs of recovery both mentally and physically. Eventually I was able to get through a whole day with a minimum amount of pain medicine and then eventually had a drug free day. That was a big accomplishment! Far from being dependent on the medication, I was eager to get off it. It was a great day when I did not need to swallow any pills.

How could I possibly hold a grudge when clearly my kitten was praying for forgiveness?

So 2 seasons, 3 surgeries, 4 months, and 12 lbs. later, I was finally able to walk free of aids! Slowly I began to put weight on my foot and was in the early stages of walking again. This was fantastic!

Shortly after this, I was fitted with custom orthotics as the ordeal had changed a few things for me. These helped to keep my feet and knees in alignment which also helped the lower back too. I sometimes forget that it's all connected - pain here can originate from there. I also learned that massage and stretching is often the best prescription for most muscular discomfort.

I also found myself being more aware of my thoughts. I was quick to weed out negative ones and nurture positive ones. I avoided indulging in "I cannot" or "It's too hard." I focused on what I was gaining and not on what I had lost. Gratitude was becoming a significant part of my attitude.

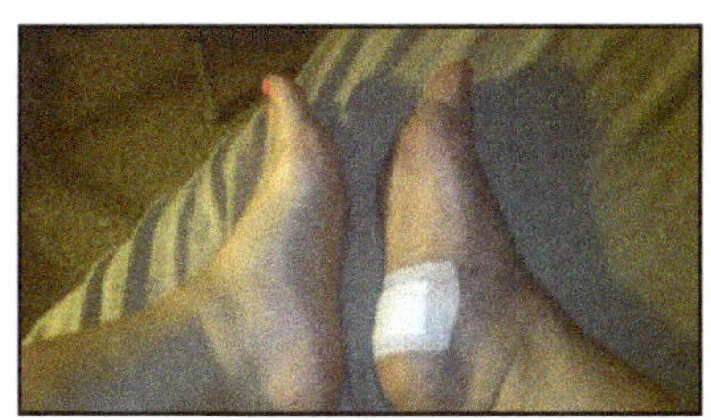

Equality is SO important!

As my mobility returned and the use of *both* feet, I was finally safe to drive again. That in itself was an indescribable pleasure! I love driving. It was a privilege that I greatly missed, and was so happy to have reinstated.

Eventually – stilettos!

Another area where I stepped up to the plate was in the area of stretching, which, prior to rewiring my LRC, I had not been doing. My leg muscles, in particular, were in very bad condition as I had not walked properly for over four months. Any massage therapist will testify to how important stretching is for overall well-being, but all the more so after recovering from an injury. I always knew that, but I struggle sometimes with procrastination. So

I started reaching for my exercise mat and played songs on YouTube like "Fields of Gold", "Over the Rainbow" and other such masterpieces by Eva Cassidy. Her voice is hauntingly beautiful and sets the perfect mood for stretching and self care. Slowly my body became more limber and healthy. It will however be an ongoing effort to make stretching a regular part of my day instead of just when I *have* to.

Eventually I regained my musical *interest* that usually complements my husband's musical *talent*. He plays several instruments all of which are in our living room and serve as a pleasant reminder every day. I picked up my guitar again and tinkered around. I wrote a few parodies and even a few old songs came back to life. I also worked on a craft project that I had wanted to do for many years. Picasso once said "Art washes away from the soul, the dust of everyday life." Hard not to agree that most creative outlets are refreshing for the soul!

Perhaps the biggest response that I had to this crisis, was the decision to write this book! It may have taken years to blend the plethora of details together, and quite frankly some life lessons are still busy learning, but I finally completed it! I really wanted to share this story, share my insights, and those life lessons that were learned along the way. To derive meaning from this very difficult experience, to bring closure to this ordeal, is all part of the process.

I sincerely hope that my LR code concept will inspire you to think about your own Life Response Code. Essentially we all have one. The textbook name would probably be "innate disposition" or "propensity towards", or something of that nature. But I believe the questions that it can provoke is worthy of anyone's consideration (if self-improvement is their lifestyle). Who would not benefit from studying their weaknesses when under trial, or observing behavioural nuances when challenged to the core? Who would not benefit by being more mindful to compound any good thoughts or deeds so as to perpetuate them, or by learning to ask for help or an intervention if you see a need? Perhaps a great "mission statement" when experiencing trials, would be to always have in the forefront of our mind…"what good will come from this?"

If I ask myself now: 'what good came from this toothpick crisis?' The answer is clear:

I identified *and* upgraded my Life Response Code. Was going through this experience worth the upgrade? Absolutely – the ROI was significant!

It is only natural that we all have a personal belief system and mine does not believe in fate or pre-destined outcomes. What I do believe is that unforeseen occurrences befall us all and accidents can happen to *anyone, anytime, and anywhere.* It's an imperfect world filled with imperfect people. For now. I am comforted by several scriptures that talk about a time in the future where we will all be healthy as originally intended, and "no resident will say I am sick." Isaiah 33:24

Irrespective of what happens in our lives, I believe that our thoughts *and* attitudes about what happens has a much greater impact than any other contributing factor. That which we think about most can easily become our reality. Science 101 states that positive and negative energy attracts much the same.

On that important note, I make a concentrated effort to think positive thoughts everyday so that I can attract much the same. That's the secret. I might not always do it perfectly, but I am mindful of the need to monitor myself and watch where I expend my energy.

If we liken the power of our thoughts to banking activities, then we are either making deposits or withdrawals on our well being. And we all know that overdrafts are dangerous and investments should be long term.

The End…

no actually - the Beginning…

Conclusion

Thank you for sharing in this journey right to the very end!

I ***sincerely*** hope that you take away a little something from this experience. If it's a completed book on your bookshelf - then I am thrilled! If it's a life lesson or two - then I am thrilled and honoured.

As referenced in the beginning, my theme quote is from Oprah, where she said that "Lessons often come dressed up as detours and roadblocks." My five life lessons make reference to those types of detours, and to those road-blocks which eventually became stepping stones. Our individual LR Code says much about us. It reveals our blueprint as we age, as we grow, or as we're tested, but it is editable.

Sometimes it's when we're navigating through these detours that we learn the most about ourselves. And just when we think we don't need our GPS - we do! Familiarity breeds contempt they say even from within.

I would love to hear about your experiences or maybe someone you know. Perhaps you had a similar experience, a game changer, or a sudden unexpected event in your life.

Please reach out - maybe one day
I will write a sequel...

detoursanddevelopments@shaw.ca

Life Lesson #1

Really *feeling gratitude* and really *expressing* it to others, has the power to take us to a deeper level of being.

Life Lesson #2

Being more *mindful* and reaching out to those who are not well, is part of their medicine and part of their healing.

Life Lesson #3

Having "Sacred Bookends" in your life, *inspires* you to start the day and end the day in the best possible way.

Life Lesson #4

I've learned that its okay to sit with your feelings and to sit with your pain, as they are there for a *reason*. Just don't stay there too long.

Life Lesson #5

We need to take the *action* in order to get the results we want, whether we feel like it or not. Motivation comes after taking action, rarely does it come before!

About Loss

By Kimberley Holly Curry

So here it is
But now it's gone
I thought it'd be here
All along

What to do
Without this thing
I no longer smile
I no longer sing

It happened so quickly
I didn't have time
To prepare my new life
For what's no longer mine

Whether it's sight
Or whether it's sound
Loss happens quickly
But the effects are profound

I couldn't walk
But others can't see
Some get it back
Eventually

Life lesson learned
Anything can change
Be grateful for each thing
That's not re-arranged

About the Author

Kimberley Holly Curry was born and raised in a small but rather well known town of Brantford, Ontario (home of Alexander Graham Bell and Wayne Gretzky). Being surrounded by the beautiful great lakes made for many wonderful camping memories and beaching excursions, not to mention the grandeur of autumn most notable in Ontario. Being blessed with many brothers and sisters, graduating from high school and college, and several great jobs later, she headed west and pitched her tent in big sky country - Alberta.

Not surprising that she enjoys working in the career development field helping clients develop their full potential through various initiatives. She attends the University of Calgary in the Human Resource Management Program, and as a Certified MBTI Practitioner she enjoys facilitating individual assessments, client coaching, training and development, and other business initiatives.

In keeping the dream alive of being a Philanthropist one day (by helping make the lives of those less fortunate just a little bit easier), she does her little part now by volunteering in the community and loves the concept of paying it forward!

www.lifelessonsfrom.ca

Appendix

Examples of Infections Getting Out of Control....

https://www.thestar.com/life/health_wellness/2012/01/24/flesheating_disease_could_turn_deadly_in_a_matter_of_hours.html

By ISABEL TEOTONIO Life Reporter
January 24, 2012

Flesh-eating disease could turn deadly in a matter of hours

Flesh-eating disease is the medical equivalent of being struck by lightning: it's extremely rare and very tragic.

Politician Lucien Bouchard became infected with necrotizing fasciitis and lost a leg to the disease in 1994 while he was leader of the federal official opposition Bloc Québécois party.

And the fact that it moves at breakneck speed, capable of killing a healthy person in as little as 12 hours, makes it an especially frightening and intriguing disease.

"You don't have the luxury of waiting around a few days to find out what's going on," says Dr. Michael Gardam, an infectious disease specialist at University Health Network in Toronto. "You've got to jump on it right away."

The tricky thing about this bacterial infection is that typical symptoms include skin infection and flu-like aches and pains, so some patients and even doctors may not recognize what they're dealing with until it's too late.

A few years ago, one of his patients cut her index finger while peeling an apple and became infected. Days later, the infection spread up her arm, to the armpit and across the chest. She was operated on, but later succumbed to the disease.

Such tragedies are rare, says Rau, noting that even in severe cases of the disease, most people don't die. Such was the case in the winter of 1994 when Lucien Bouchard, then-leader of the Bloc Québécois, was forced to have his leg amputated because of the illness.

According to Health Canada, there are between 90 and 200 cases of necrotizing fasciitis each year, about 20 to 30 per cent of which are fatal.

One of the cardinal features of flesh-eating disease, says Gardam is that "the pain is more than you'd expect from what you're looking at."

Another Traumatic Experience

http://www.ctvnews.ca/canada/manitoba-mother-loses-three-limbs-to-strep-infection-1.3336919

By CTV Winnipeg Reporter Jon Hendricks

In early February, Cari Kirkness thought she had the flu. But her illness, which started with a sore throat, quickly spiralled out of control. Soon, the 28-year-old Manitoba mother of two had lost both legs and her right arm to an incredibly aggressive strep infection.

"Her sister bought her stuff like Advil flu, orange juice, and you know, thinking it was just a flu," her mother, Loretta Kirkness, said.

But it wasn't the flu -- it was group A streptococcus, a bacteria often found in the throat and on the skin.

According to Manitoba Health, the group A streptococcus bacteria can be responsible for a broad range of illnesses, including a simple sore throat. But in rare cases, it can also lead to invasive, serious illnesses such as necrotizing fasciitis, commonly known as the flesh-eating disease, and deadly toxic shock syndrome.

"Within 24 hours our lives just changed," Loretta said.

With her health deteriorating, Cari went to the ER, and before she knew it, surgeons were on standby.

"I realized it was serious when the doctor told me that I might lose my arm," Cari said.

Doctors quickly amputated her right arm and a leg, but Cari's conditions still wasn't improving. They soon put her into a medically induced coma. The infection, they learned, had travelled to her other leg too. To save her life, they had to amputate it too.

"Then they told us to decide what we wanted to do," Loretta said. "You have 15 minutes to decide."

The family chose life, then waited, hoping Cari would recover.

A GoFundMe page has been set up for Cari and her family. The crowdfunding campaign hopes to raise $200,000 to help with childcare costs, a wheelchair accessible van and a down payment on a one-storey home.

According to Wikipedia:

https://en.wikipedia.org/wiki/Necrotizing_fasciitis

Necrotizing fasciitis

Necrotising fasciitis (NF), commonly known as **flesh-eating disease**, is an infection that results in the death of the body›s soft tissue.[3] It is a severe disease of sudden onset that spreads rapidly. Symptoms include red or purple skin in the affected area, severe pain, fever, and vomiting.[3] The most commonly affected areas are the limbs and perineum.[2]

Please reference the website above

Typically the infection enters the body through a break in the skin such as a cut or burn.[3] Risk factors include poor immune function such as from diabetes or cancer, obesity, alcoholism, intravenous drug use, and peripheral vascular disease.[2][3] It is not typically spread between people.[3] The disease is classified into four types, depending on the infecting organism. Between 55% and 80% of cases involve more than one type of bacteria. Methicillin-resistant *Staphylococcus aureus* (MRSA) is involved in up to a third of cases. Medical imaging is helpful to confirm the diagnosis.[4]

Prevention is by good wound care and handwashing.[3] It is usually treated with surgery to remove the infected tissue and intravenous antibiotics.[2][3] Often a combination of antibiotics are used such as penicillin G, clindamycin, vancomycin, and gentamicin.[2] Delays in surgery are associated with a higher risk of death.[4] Despite high quality treatment the risk of death is between 25% and 35%.[2]

Necrotizing fasciitis affects 0.4 to 1 person per 100,000 per year.[4] Both sexes are affected equally.[2] It becomes more common among older people and is very rare in children.[4] Necrotizing fasciitis has been described at least since the time of Hippocrates.[2] The term «necrotising fasciitis» first came into use in 1952.[4][5]

Signs and Symptoms

People usually complain of intense pain that may seem excessive given the external appearance of the skin. People initially have signs of inflammation, fever and a fast heart rate. With progression of the disease, often within hours, tissue becomes progressively swollen, the skin becomes discolored and develops blisters. Crepitus may be present and there may be a discharge of fluid, said to resemble «dish-water». Diarrhea and vomiting are also common symptoms.

In the early stages, signs of inflammation may not be apparent if the bacteria are deep within the tissue. If they are *not* deep, signs of inflammation, such as redness and swollen or hot skin, develop very quickly. Skin color may progress to violet, and blisters may form, with subsequent necrosis (death) of the subcutaneous tissues.

Furthermore, people with necrotizing fasciitis typically have a fever and appear sick. Mortality rates are as high as 73 percent if left untreated.[6] Without surgery and medical assistance, such as antibiotics, the infection will rapidly progress and will eventually lead to death.[7]

So as we can see with just a handful of articles and references - infections are dangerous! They might start out small and seemingly harmless, but some can result in amputations or even be deadly! Note to self - keep it clean!

Photo Gallery

WARNING

Some images may be disturbing to some readers.

Image 1 on page 40

Seven days after the 1st Surgery-not looking too good

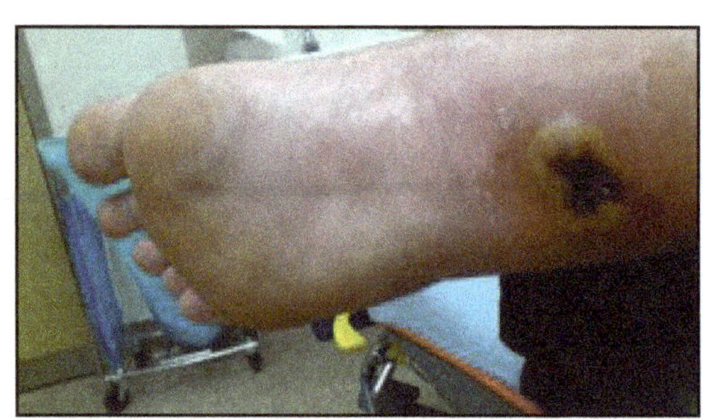

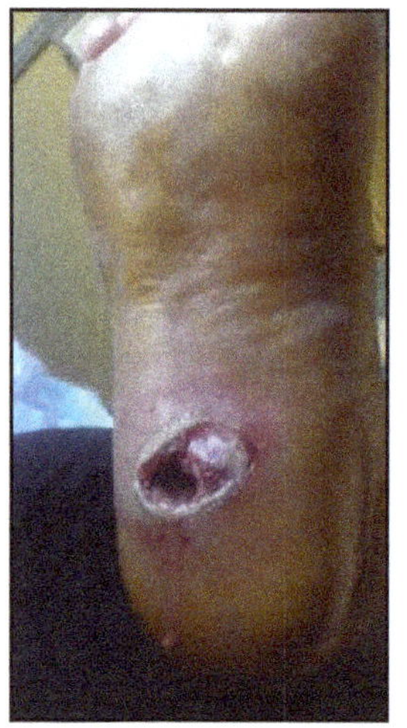

Image 2 on page 49

My foot didn't much like the 2nd surgery either

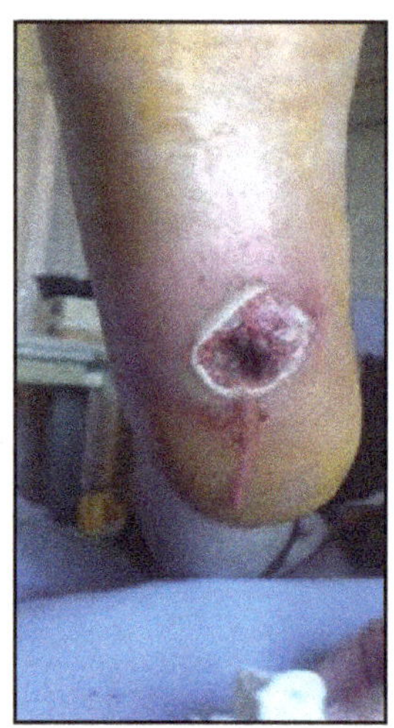

Image 3 on page 56

Looking a little angry!

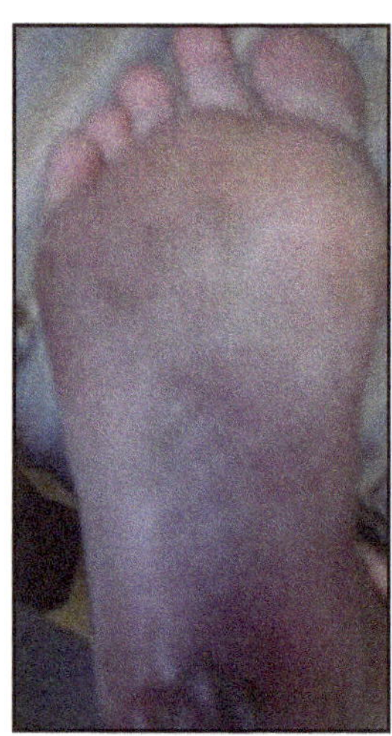

Image 4 on page 64

Roses are red and feet are blue

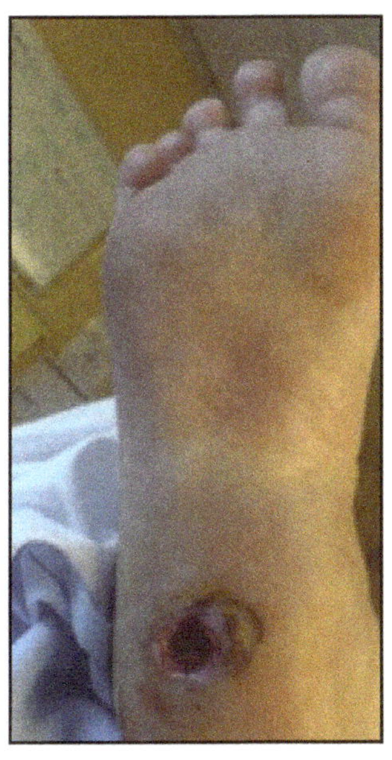

Image 5 on page 84

Just one more surgery

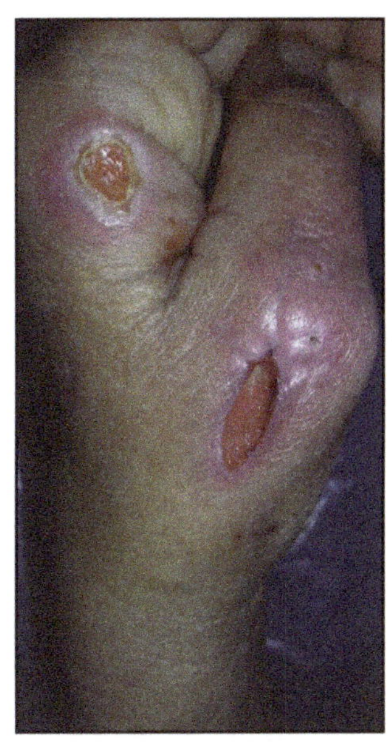

Image 6 on page 98

She wasn't expecting that after cleaning!

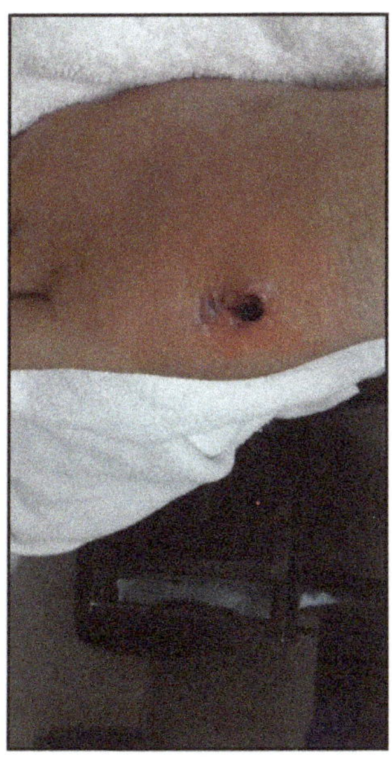

Image 7 on page 99

Just an everyday Australian spider bite!

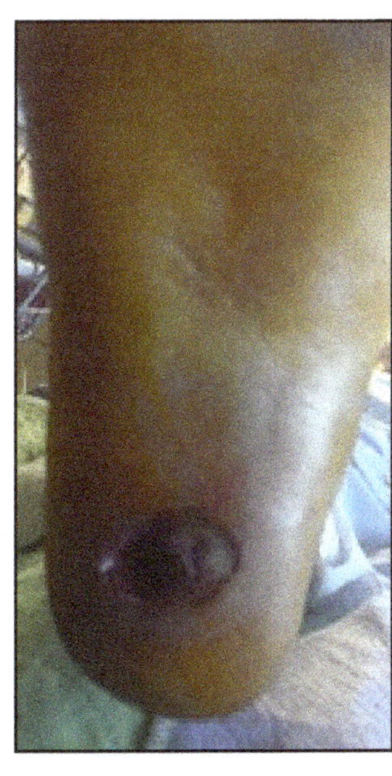

Image 8 on page 103

Looking *almost* good to go

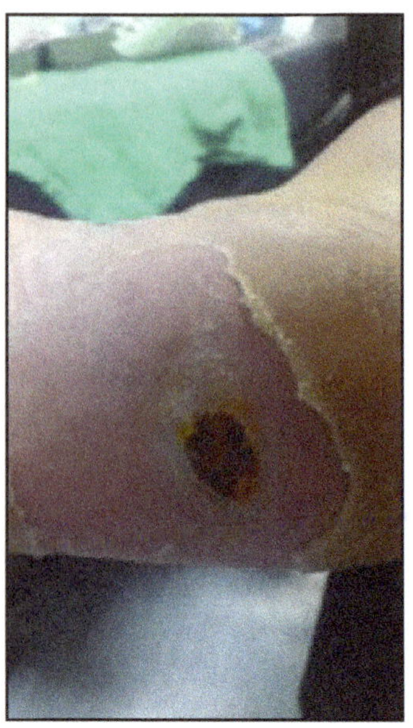

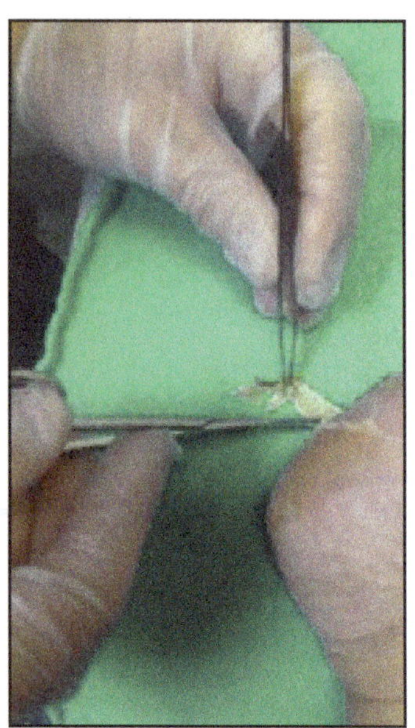

Images 9 and 10 on page 113

Even my pedicure became
a medical procedure!

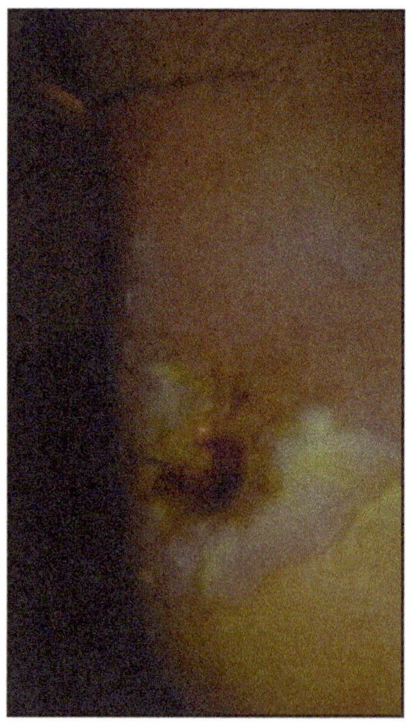

Image 11 on page 118

Evidently keeping the wound
dry is paramount to healing

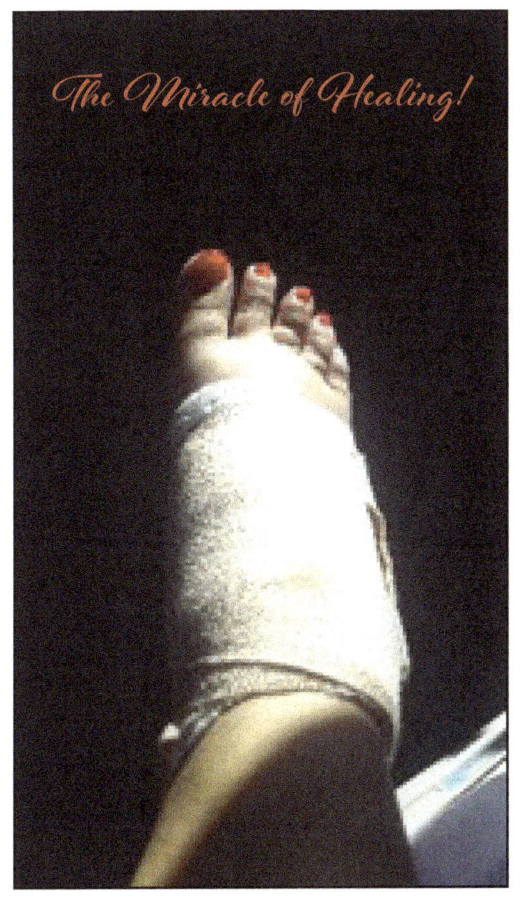
The Miracle of Healing!

CPSIA information can be obtained
at www.ICGtesting.com
Printed in the USA
LVHW07s1938200918
590814LV00007B/26/P